First published in the United Kingdom 2

Serendipity
Suite 530
37 Store Street
Bloomsbury
London
WC1E 7QF

This edition

Copyright ©
Robert Body 2013

All rights reserved. No part of this book may be reprinted or reproduced or utilized in any form or by any electronic, mechanical or other means, now known or hereafter invented, including photocopying, scanning and recording, or in any information storage or retrieval system without the permission in writing from the publisher.

ISBN 978-1-291-55872-2

TAKING THE WINGS OF THE MORNING

INDEX

ACKNOWLEDGEMENTS	1
FOREWORD	4
PROLOGUE	6
THE FIRST BEGINNING	7
THE SECOND BEGINNING	15
FROM TRAINEE TO DFC	25
THE MIDDLE PERIOD	52
MORE INFORMATION, AND THE RECOVERY OF FK790	56
THE TEMPSFORD MONTHS	81
5/6 JULY 1944	108
AFTER THE CRASH & SASKIA SPIEL	135
THE SECOND ENDING	145
WAS THAT THE END?	158
GLOSSARY	162

TAKING THE WINGS OF THE MORNING

ACKNOWLEDGEMENTS

TAKING THE WINGS OF THE MORNING

There are many people and organizations who have been of enormous assistance in obtaining the information regarding all aspects of the story.

From the Netherlands I would like to extend my deepest thanks to Klaas Groeneveld and family, Klaasje Bilsma and Annie Bockma for their help and hospitality. Huub van Sabben and Aad Neeven, the Dutch researchers, have never ceased to amaze me with their knowledge about the activities of the SOE in the Netherlands and details of operations. Without their persistent cajoling this book would never have been written. Also I would like to thank so many others whose efforts were vital, the salvage teams and divers, the aircraft recovery team and all those who doggedly worked at proving the identity of the remains found in FK790. The Directors of the Kazematten Museum who have spent so much time in creating a permanent display honouring those on board the aircraft. The people of Exmorra who have one of the propellers mounted, as a monument, in their village. Cees Scheepvart who let me have copies of documents written by his father, Albert, who played a vital part in the days following the crash.

My thanks go to The Commonwealth War Graves Commission, RAF Insworth, Lt. Col. Le Hardy and Ms. Vicky Bant of the Defence section of the British Embassy in The Hague whose hard work brought everything to a smooth and moving conclusion. Also to those from the Tempsford Squadrons who have helped, supported and encouraged me during the last few years; especially Air Chief Marshall Sir Lewis Hodges, Ron Morris (who was also flying a Hudson on a mission to Holland on the 5/6 July '44) and Mr. L Smith DFC who gave me information about life on the squadron.

Mr. C Cutbush kindly translated many pages of the documents I had; my wife Helen who put up with papers and copies of records seemingly strewn all over the house and has had to act as editor and proof reader.

There are many others, too numerous to mention, who helped in all manner of ways including spotting my typing errors and some early proof reading; you all know who you are and I offer my thanks.

FOREWORD

In the quiet, ancient Church of England in Tempsford there are memorials to the two RAF Squadrons – No 138 and No 161 - which operated from the nearby RAF Station which took its name from the village. There is also a Book of Remembrance containing the names of 623 airmen who gave their lives in the pursuit of their operational objectives. Included in that list are the names of the crew of Hudson FK790 (MA-R) lost over Holland on the night of 5/6 June 1944. The pilot was F/Lt J W Menzies DFC, the uncle of the author, Bob Body.

When Bob Body's mother died in January 1985, Bob became the proud owner of his uncle's medals. Since then he has spent years trying to establish his uncle's contribution to the war, especially as F/Lt Menzies had "no known grave" and his name was listed amongst the many thousands at the RAF Memorial at Runnymede.

Progress for Bob was very slow and at times extremely frustrating, but in 1997 came the breakthrough when the remains of Hudson FK790 were raised from the waters of the Ijsselmeer. Parts of FK790 are now on display at Exmorra and the Kazematten Museum, Kornwandersand, in Northern Holland. Bob has received endless help and tremendous kindness from numerous people in Holland - Aad Neeven and Huub Van Sabben, both historical researchers, to name but two.

The four young airmen who perished in FK790 now lie side by side in the Commonwealth War Graves Section of the United Reformed Church in Makkum, in Northern Holland; not very far from the Museum at Kornwandersand where Bob's uncle's medals are now proudly displayed.

The people of Holland have nothing but the deepest admiration and gratitude for the work of these two Wartime Squadrons, expressions of which I was to receive personally on their "Liberation Day Remembrance" on 4 May 2003 at a Memorial of their own "Fallen Agents" at Scheveningen near The Hague.

I can only congratulate Bob Body (and his wife, Helen) on an excellent work of detection, even if in the end questions still remain unanswered.

RON MORRIS

F/Lt R Morris DFC NVK

PROLOGUE

In writing this book I have set out, in part, to document the career of my uncle, Flt/Lt J. W. Menzies DFC, with the RAF and, also, to relate the curious tale, of luck and coincidence, as to how much of this information was gathered. I have asked many people as to how I should start this task. Almost all have said "Start at the beginning and finish at the end". "Well," you may say, "that sounds perfectly reasonable and easy enough." In reply I would ask: "How do you start a story that has *two* beginnings?" Furthermore: "How do you finish a story that, on the one hand has ended and yet, on the other, has not?"

Let me explain. Beginning one really starts at the birth of my uncle, for without this there would be no story at all. Beginning two is when I started to trace his history with the RAF. What I mean by the two different endings will, I believe, become obvious as the story draws to its close.

AND THOUGH NO STORY MAY TELL
THEIR NAME, THEIR WORK THEIR GLORY
THEY REST IN HEARTS THAT LOVE THEM WELL
THEIR GRACE THEIR COUNTRY'S STORY

THE FIRST BEGINNING

TAKING THE WINGS OF THE MORNING

John Watherston Menzies, known as Ian to the family, and from here on referred to as Ian, was born in Croydon on 19 May 1916. He was born into a prosperous middle class family and became the middle child of three, two girls and a boy. The two sisters were named Ann and Mona; Ann was to become my mother.

I know very little of Ian as a person as he was killed before I was born. I believe that his death had such an impact on my mother that she very rarely mentioned him. I am sure that she never really came to terms with his being reported missing in 1944. However, I shall share with you the small amount of information I have gathered about him over the years for the period up to his joining the RAF; from there we will explore his RAF career and the events leading up to his remains being found.

Ian was educated at Epsom college. It would appear that while here he was a keen and proficient sportsman. Pictures from the family albums show him in cricket whites alongside a colleague, the caption saying "Captain and Vice-captain."

However, I would question his proficiency; one day, when alerted to a fast approaching cricket ball by the cry of "Catch" he turned and, sure enough caught it - not in his hands but full on the nose. Various other photographs in the family albums show him with golf clubs and tennis racquets. Probably a safer option.

Ian is on the right

From half remembered conversations with my mother I seem to recall Ian being very interested in aircraft and flying. Living in Croydon, as they did, Ian would have had plenty of opportunity to observe aircraft in action, both during routine flying, and at the air shows that were held at the nearby Croydon Aerodrome. Once again, my belief that he had a very

TAKING THE WINGS OF THE MORNING

keen interest in flying is supported by pictures from the family album.

On 8 December 1939 he enlisted at Eltham in London, his papers showing "Trade on Enlistment" as "Insurance Inspector". At this time he would have been with the Atlas Insurance Company in London; whether this had been his only employment after full-time education I do not know.

After a short period of initial training he was posted to No 162 Officer Cadet Training Unit at Bulford In Wiltshire. From a letter home dated 28 July 1940 it would appear that war was still a great adventure to be enjoyed; he wrote to his mother, saying "I was on guard here on Friday night and at about 12.30 there were all sorts of fun and games going on in the sky - searchlights - German planes - bombs - anti- aircraft fire. None, however were close enough to be exciting". Little did he know then just how "exciting" things would become in the not too distant future.

Upon completion of his training at 162 OCTU Ian joined, on 28 September 1940, the 2nd Battalion of the North Staffordshire Regiment with the rank of 2nd Lieutenant.

A year went past, and during that time it is obvious that his interest in aircraft and flying was still as strong as ever; on 30 September 1941 his dreams of flying were realised. He had volunteered for the RAF and had been granted a commission as a Pilot Officer in the Royal Air Force Volunteer Reserve.

Some seven months of training then followed; first at No 12 Service Flying Training School and then with No 19 Operational Training Unit. From here his flying then took him through promotion to Flight Lieutenant, a tour of duties with Bomber Command, meeting the King to receive his DFC, Target Towing and finally to a Special Duties Squadron.

On the night of 5/6 July 1944 he took off on a mission. The following day the family received the much dreaded "PRIORITY" Post Office Telegram. This stated, quite bluntly, " Regret to inform you that your son Flt/Lt J W Menzies is reported missing................" Enclosed with the telegram was the standard ADVICE TO THE RELATIVE OF A MAN WHO IS MISSING which, I presume, was supposed to offer some crumb of comfort and hope. Maybe it did.

…

TAKING THE WINGS OF THE MORNING

From receipt of the telegram there followed a period of 11 months, which must have seemed interminable; not knowing what had happened, not knowing where he had gone missing and, of course, all the time hoping and praying that news would arrive that Ian was safe, perhaps a prisoner. This was not to be. On 4 June 1945 a letter was received from the Air Ministry stating "that in view of the lapse of time, and the absence of further news of your son, Flt/Lt J W Menzies, since the date he was reported missing they must regretfully conclude that he has lost his life."

With that letter the relatives were left to deal with the formalities of death. All the necessary paperwork, will, bank accounts, tax etcetera. While dealing with these matters they did not even have the comfort of knowing that he had been properly laid to rest; there was no body to bury.

I am convinced that until the day my mother died she still hoped that perhaps he had crashed and lost his memory, and that one day it would come back and he would return. Was this too much to hope? Was it a ridiculous dream? Surely not; there had been no body so there must be a chance.

The only monument to Ian's short life was the recording of his name carved in stone, along with 20 thousand other airmen who have no known grave, at the RAF Memorial at Runnymede. An imposing building, set in beautifully landscaped gardens, overlooking the Thames Valley, where peace and tranquillity prevail. At the centre of the memorial, facing out over the valley, is a large glass window which has beautifully engraved on panels the words of Psalm 139, some of which I believe are very pertinent to Ian's story.

> *If I take the wings of the morning: and*
> *Remain in the uttermost parts of the sea;*
> *Even there also shall Thy hand lead me:*
> *And Thy right hand shall hold me.*

Unfortunately, Ian's parents and my mother all died before the story could be concluded.

TAKING THE WINGS OF THE MORNING

THE SECOND BEGINNING

TAKING THE WINGS OF THE MORNING

On 31 January 1985 my mother died and I inherited Ian's medals along with some photographs of him, and the few personal belongings that had been returned to the family. The belongings included a small wallet, a silver ID bracelet, an old "Dog Tag" and a photograph of a young lady - more about her later. Added to these personal items were a few papers from the Air Ministry and some letters to and from his mother. All in all not very much to show for the years he lived, and certainly not many clues as to his time with the RAF.

I had always had a deep interest in Ian, and what had happened all those years ago, although during the time I was growing up at home the only reminders, in the house, of his existence were a couple of small portrait photographs and a little display box containing his DFC. While I often enquired about him little was said. So now that I had these few possessions I decided to attempt to piece together as much of his history as possible. Had I known then that it was to take 15 years to gather together the information, (which will unfold as I tell his story), I am not sure that I would have started. However, I did, and along the way I have made many good friends and met many interesting people both in this country and in Holland.

TAKING THE WINGS OF THE MORNING

Having no experience of historical research, and not even having Ian's service number, I did not have a clear idea as to where I should start. A few telephone calls to various museums led me to write to RAF Personnel at Insworth in Gloucestershire. I had been told that this was the place where all the records were kept, so having posted my letter I sat back, feeling very pleased with myself for being so successful in my quest, and waited for the expected parcel of documents to drop through the letterbox and onto the mat. Ha! This research stuff was easy!

Time passed and sure enough I got a reply from Insworth; not the parcel of detailed information I had hoped for, but a short list of Ian's postings and duties. Along with this, I am pleased to say, was a copy of the citation for the award of the Distinguished Flying Cross. Still not much to go on but at least some progress. The list of postings and Squadron numbers was, in fact, the starting place for all that was to come, by sign posting the various avenues of enquiries that needed to be pursued.

Looking back now I did very little at the time to follow up on the small progress I had made and really just let the matter drop, until a day, maybe a year or two later. I had to make a business visit to the museum at Tangmere. Once the purpose of my visit was over I started to have a look at the museum and mentioned to the curator that my uncle had been posted missing while serving with 161 Squadron. I now think that it was his reply that spurred me on to find out more about Ian's service time, for his reply was "Oh, he was with one of the funny squadrons, the cloak and dagger boys," I asked him what he meant by this and he then explained that 161 Squadron was a Special Duties squadron. By this he meant that they delivered agents into occupied territory either by parachute or, sometimes, by a night landing in a lonely field.

Like many people who, when about to read a book, skip to the back pages for a peek to see "Who Dunnit", I decided to start with Ian's service with 161 Squadron. Surely as this was a Special Duties squadron this would be the most interesting and as it was the most recent part of his time with the RAF perhaps the easiest to find out about.

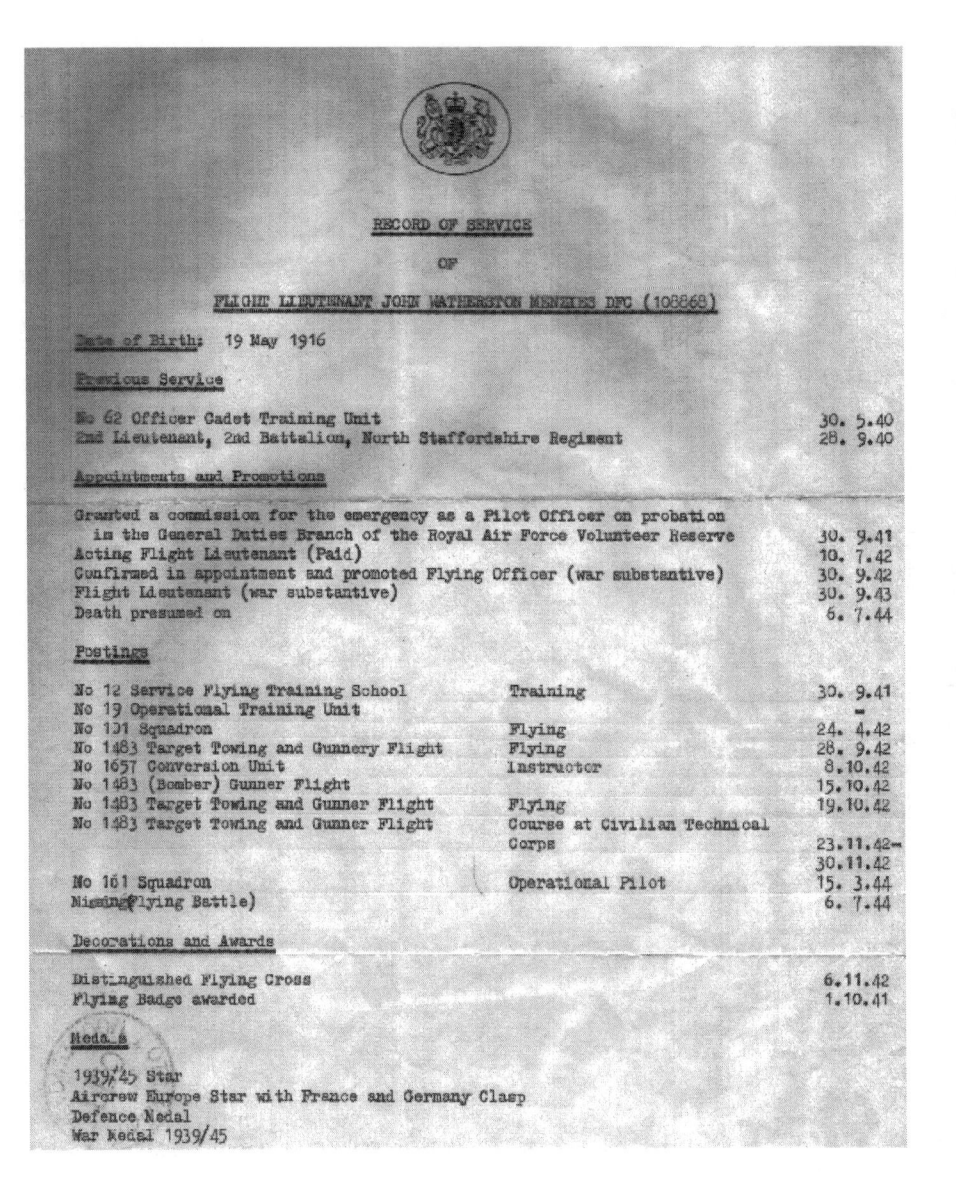

RECORD OF SERVICE

OF

FLIGHT LIEUTENANT JOHN WATHERSTON MENZIES DFC (108868)

Date of Birth: 19 May 1916

Previous Service

No 62 Officer Cadet Training Unit	30. 5.40
2nd Lieutenant, 2nd Battalion, North Staffordshire Regiment	28. 9.40

Appointments and Promotions

Granted a commission for the emergency as a Pilot Officer on probation in the General Duties Branch of the Royal Air Force Volunteer Reserve	30. 9.41
Acting Flight Lieutenant (Paid)	10. 7.42
Confirmed in appointment and promoted Flying Officer (war substantive)	30. 9.42
Flight Lieutenant (war substantive)	30. 9.43
Death presumed on	6. 7.44

Postings

No 12 Service Flying Training School	Training	30. 9.41
No 19 Operational Training Unit		—
No 131 Squadron	Flying	24. 4.42
No 1483 Target Towing and Gunnery Flight	Flying	28. 9.42
No 1657 Conversion Unit	Instructor	8.10.42
No 1483 (Bomber) Gunner Flight		15.10.42
No 1483 Target Towing and Gunner Flight	Flying	19.10.42
No 1483 Target Towing and Gunner Flight	Course at Civilian Technical Corps	23.11.42–30.11.42
No 161 Squadron	Operational Pilot	15. 3.44
Missing (Flying Battle)		6. 7.44

Decorations and Awards

Distinguished Flying Cross	6.11.42
Flying Badge awarded	1.10.41

Medals

1939/45 Star
Aircrew Europe Star with France and Germany Clasp
Defence Medal
War Medal 1939/45

Record of Service

The first port of call was the local library to see what others had written on the subject of Special Duties Squadrons. I found three or four books that had Ian's name in them and said that his aircraft had gone missing. So, nothing new here, although in an odd sort of way it was very pleasing to see his name in print. However, I must admit that I felt somewhat deflated by the lack of instant success and as a result my enthusiasm was severely dampened and I put the project on hold.

I cannot, now, remember how long I let the project just lie dormant; it was certainly many months, if not a year or more, before I decided to resume my quest for information. The next attempt was to look for information on the Special Operations Executive (SOE). This was the group that controlled the agents. Once again several visits to the local library yielded interesting information but not what I was after; what I did notice were many references to the Public Record Office (PRO) at Kew as the source of much of the material contained in the various books. So this was the key that I was looking for, just ring up the PRO, tell them what I was after and Hey Presto - they would send it to me. In due course I rang and started to put my request to them, only to be told that while they could understand what I wanted to happen, that was not the way things worked. They told me I had to go to Kew and search for this information for myself. I should have known that my idea was too simple. So, armed with paper and pens it was off to Kew for Helen, my wife, and me.

TAKING THE WINGS OF THE MORNING

Perhaps I should include a word of caution for the benefit of anyone visiting the Public Record Office (now the National Archives) for the first time. The systems at Kew make the finding of documents as easy as possible and the friendly and patient staff are very willing to guide the beginner through the system. The only problem that I found was that I was totally overwhelmed by the amount of information that is available, not just about the RAF in WW2 but on so many other diverse topics. It was like a sweet-toothed child being given the run of the confectionery store. There were just so many good things to be had that the problem was to make a start and not get side-tracked; I am sure that anyone who has been there will endorse this.

A plan of action was formulated. We knew which Squadrons Ian had flown with so we needed to find their diaries, starting with the latest and then working backwards. Well, this seemed a good idea but, yet again, my hopes of an early and easy success were soon dashed. I did not really know how or where to begin the task I had set myself and it appeared to me that despite my best efforts I seemed to be coming up against a brick wall all the time. I assumed that this was because the work that Ian had been involved with was so secret. In fact many of the files I wanted to see *were* still covered by the 50 year rule and therefore not open to the public. With the benefit of hindsight I now see how disjointed and haphazard my search efforts were.

Helen, my wife, came to my aid. She had graduated in History and, therefore, had a much better knowledge of how to go about matters than I did. A letter to her professor at the University of East Anglia, explaining, what had now become *our* problems, soon elicited a reply. The professor wrote saying that he had forwarded her letter to one of his other students who ".. had spent some time in the RAF and proved to be a bottomless well of information about the military history and intelligence operations of the last war." Eventually we had a reply from this mature student which in a fairly blunt way, said that the lack of progress was not that the information was not available but rather I had not a clue how to go about getting it or decipher what I had. "Thank you!" I thought, that much I *have* worked out for myself.

Clearly with the current approach to this research we were having little, if indeed any, success. We therefore decided to go back and concentrate our efforts at the beginning of Ian's service with the RAF, and hope that as time went on, with more experience under our belts, by the time we got to the 1944 period our efforts would be better rewarded.

Very little was found regarding his time in training with NO 12 SFTS and No 19 OTU other than general information. So the next move was to look for 101 Squadron. This proved to be much easier; squadron records, for the time that Ian was with the squadron, were located without difficulty. It was now a simple matter, though very time consuming, to go through the records held on microfilm and select the information we wanted. Clearly laid out on the film were the details of the operations Ian flew as, first, the second pilot and later, the captain of the aircraft. To me this information was very interesting but it really was just plain, cold hard facts. Details of Takeoff Times, Time over Target, Bomb Loads, while very important facts do not make for interesting reading and do not, by themselves, give any feeling for what life would have been like on a day to day basis with a bomber squadron. What this meant was that although we had now started to uncover some of the information we required, it made us only too aware of just how much more there was to do to get a proper understanding of just what he did in that period.

Looking over the information that has now been gathered, over a period of more than 15 years, arriving in no particular order, sometimes in great chunks but more often than not as small unconnected items, it becomes apparent that, for ease of explanation and reading, Ian's career may be separated into three periods.

1. From joining the RAF, through training and to the end of his time with 101 Squadron.

TAKING THE WINGS OF THE MORNING

2. The period between leaving 101 Squadron, through Coastal Command, Target Towing and up to joining 161 Squadron.

3. The last section covering his service with 161 Squadron and the final mission, the quest for more information on this period and the events following the recovery of his remains.

TAKING THE WINGS OF THE MORNING

FROM TRAINEE TO DFC

30 September 1941 - 27 September 1942

Flying Officer Kite, drawn by Ian

TAKING THE WINGS OF THE MORNING

This stage of Ian's career was relatively easy to trace now that we had a bit more experience, although the search methods were the same. We now had a better idea of how and where to search. We were now more disciplined in our approach; well at least Helen was. I am afraid that I was then, and still remain, a bit of a "butterfly" when it comes to the routine of searching. I will flit from one interesting topic to another with scant regard as to whether or not they are linked or, indeed, if they are even relevant.

Delving through the records at Kew turned up valuable information in way of Operational Record Books, Squadron and Station diaries. 101 Squadron, now based at RAF Brize Norton, were kind enough to search their records and assisted us by supplying copies of all the battle orders covering Ian's operations with them, both as second pilot and, later, as pilot. Through the 101 Squadron Association we were able to trace one member who flew with Ian, as his rear gunner, in July 1942 and who was kind enough to talk with us.

Unfortunately, we were not so lucky with obtaining information regarding the very early part of his career, with No 12 Flying Training School and then No 19 Operational Training Unit.

No 12 Flying Training School - Grantham

Ian was posted here on 30 September 1941 and, so far, from the records I have seen, I have been unable to find any report or document that mentions him by name. Neither is there any clear indication how long he was stationed here. His service record shows that from 12 FTS he progressed to No 19 OTU (Operational Training Unit) but no date has been entered for this.

I have taken just a few snippets from the records for October 1941, a period when Ian must have been there.

On 11 October, a pupil, along with his flying instructor, managed to down a JU88 when their Oxford, on night flying training, collided with it. Sadly both the sergeant instructor and the pupil were killed. This appears to have been the most significant event of the month.

The next event, in order of apparent importance, was the arrival of 75 Sticky Grenades; on 24 October, the entry in the records is "Practice at throwing grenades". Perhaps this was more exciting than the other task for the day, "Work on digging trenches". Maybe the trenches should have been dug before the practice throwing of grenades!

One thing we do know is that Ian made good use of the mess here and paid his bills promptly (September's bill is receipted on the 1st October). From his bill for September it appears that he used most of the facilities provided by the mess, some more than others. With only 3d (about 1.5p) and 2d (1p) being spent on P.S.I Sports Subscription and Telephone calls respectively one can only surmise that he did not feel the need for exercise nor the inclination to call someone to talk about it.

19 OTU - Forres

As mentioned previously, I have not been able to find any clear reference to Ian during his time here and neither does his service record show a date for his transfer from No 12 SFTS. The only fact I have is that he graduated, if that is an appropriate term, from 19 OTU and joined 101 Squadron, at Bourn, in Cambridgeshire, on 24 April 1942 as a Pilot Officer.

TAKING THE WINGS OF THE MORNING

101 SQUADRON
24 April 1942 - 27 September 1942

Four days after arriving on the Squadron, based at Bourn in Cambridgeshire, Ian was on operations, with Kiel as the target. Flying as second pilot to Sqdn/Ldr Watts they were one of eighty-eight aircraft that attacked the shipyards that night.

The entry in Bomber Command War Diaries, by Martin Middlebrook and Chris Everitt, says "the Kiel records show that damage was caused to all of the 3 shipyards, to the hospital of the Naval Academy and to the university library as well as to private housing". Squadron Leader Watts was forced to return early after abandoning his mission due to the engines overheating. He arrived safely back at Bourn with the bomb load intact.

The following night Ian was on operations again, this time as second pilot to Sgt Llewellyn. The target was the Gnome and Rhone aero-engine factory just outside Paris. The records of 101 Squadron for that night state that the objective was clearly identified in conditions of excellent visibility and that fierce fires, punctuated with blue flashes and explosions, were seen across the factory buildings. Two of the crews taking part in the raid were very disturbed to find some of their bombs "hung up" when they landed back at base.

In May 1942 Ian was only involved in one raid, on Hamburg, still flying as second pilot to Sgt Llewellyn. This took place on the third of the month, the hundredth anniversary of a great fire in the city. If Bomber Command hoped to replicate this event I think that they were unsuccessful. Reported as completely burnt out were a large entertainment palace, a theatre and a cinema (all in the Reeperbahn area) and a dock side warehouse full of goods and vehicles. However, once again, the aircraft was forced to return early, this time because of a faulty radio.

TAKING THE WINGS OF THE MORNING

May also saw the first of the "Thousand Bomber" Raids. Twelve aircraft from 101 Squadron joined this raid to Cologne, two of them failing to return. One of the pictures that I found amongst Ian's possessions was a picture of a Wellington bomber, number X3670, and a group of airmen standing and seated alongside it. Why this picture was among his personal effects and what significance it may have had for him I do not know. I do know, however, that this aircraft and crew were lost on the Cologne raid.

As I can find no mention of Ian for the rest of May, I believe it is reasonable to assume that his time would have been taken up with further training, most likely cross-country work, night flying training and, possibly, formation flying. This belief is supported by the fact that on 27 May he was transferred out of the squadron to No 1502 BAT flight at Wyton, from which he returned to the squadron on 2 June. BAT was the abbreviation for Beam Approach Training, the idea being to train the pilots for instrument landings. I believe that, at times, their cockpit windscreens were blanked out to make the training more realistic!

June seems to have been a quiet month with only two operational sorties flown by Ian and his crew; one to Emden and the other to Bremen. On the Emden raid Ian flew as second pilot to Flt/Lt Osborn, who was on his second tour of duty. Again the aircraft had to return early, this time the cause was a combination of engine and Inter-Com trouble.

July saw a significant increase in the number of operations carried out by Ian and his crew, with a total for the month of six. These comprised one on Wilhelmshaven, three on Duisberg, one on Saarbrucken and one on Dusseldorf.

8 July saw their first raid of that month, on Wilhelmshaven; Ian again flew as second pilot to his Wing Commander, W/C Eaton. It was at about this time that the period for which new pilots had to fly as second pilot was dramatically reduced. The powers that be had realised that having two trained pilots aboard one aircraft was not a particularly good idea as this increased the damage done to the RAF if that aircraft was shot down. From now on Ian was to captain his own aircraft; a Wellington III X3457- letter P.

According to some of the general records the first four of July's raids, Wilhelmshaven and Duisberg, were not particularly successful for various reasons, with the bombing falling away from the target areas and into open countryside. In the ORB (Operational Record Book) of 101 Squadron there is an entry for the raid on Duisberg on 25 July which, perhaps, goes against the general trend. The entry states that 101 Squadron crews attacked Duisberg, the target being illuminated by fires. Two of the aircraft carried 4,000lb bombs. Sergeant Foxcroft reported that he was confident that his "beautiful bomb" exploded near the fire.

The last raid of the month, on Dusseldorf with 630 aircraft taking part, was indeed a heavy one. For the first time there were over one hundred Lancasters taking part along with three hundred and eight Wellingtons, plus Stirlings, Halifaxes and Hampdens. In excess of 900 tons of bombs were dropped that night. Ian and his crew took-off at 00.15 and returned, safely, four and a quarter hours later at 04:30.

Martin Middlebrook & Chris Everitt's Bomber Command War Diaries say that the records kept by Dusseldorf were very detailed and reported that some 453 buildings, in and around Dusseldorf, were destroyed. Hundreds of fires were started and many people killed. The report from Dusseldorf even gives details of a cow with an injured udder!

On 8 July 1942, Sgt Wade joined Ian's crew, as the rear gunner, for some Beam Approach work at Wyton. He was to fly with him several more times during the month, on both training and operational flights.

Through the 101 Squadron Association I have been able to trace Mr. Wade and have been able to talk to him on a number of occasions.

Sergeant Wade, who went on to become Flt/Lt Wade DFC had a remarkable story to tell, although only a tiny part of it directly concerned his time with Ian. He flew in excess of two tours of operations, over 60 missions, an astounding achievement for a rear gunner, a position that carried a life expectancy that was measured in weeks rather than months, let alone years. I think that the short life expectancy is poignantly made in a poem by R. W. Gilbert:

Requiem for an Air-Gunner

The pain has stopped,
For I am dead.
My time on earth is done.
But in a hundred years from now,
I'll still be twenty-one.

My brief sweet life is over,
My eyes no longer see,
No summer walks,
No Christmas trees,
No pretty girls for me.

TAKING THE WINGS OF THE MORNING

I've got the chop, I've had it.
My nightly ops are done.
Yet in another hundred years,
I'll still be twenty-one.

I asked Mr. Wade how he came to be flying with Ian for that month and he told me that Ian had been asking for a gunner, as his had been posted out, and so Sgt Wade had volunteered to fly with him. Mr. Wade made a point of saying that one was not made to fly with anybody so, if one had any doubts, for whatever reason, it was quite in order to refuse to fly with the person looking for crew. Mr. Wade went on to say that, although he did not know Ian well, he had a good reputation amongst the aircrew as a competent pilot, and he therefore had no qualms when it came to volunteering to fly with him.

While looking through the ORB for 101 Squadron I found this entry for 8 May 1942 regarding a raid on Warnemunde. "............Flt. Lt. Machin returned early with sickness after jettisoning his bombs off SYLT. His rear gunner Sgt WADE ably assisted him in flying the aircraft safely back to base".

TAKING THE WINGS OF THE MORNING

Mr. Wade explained to me just what had happened that night. On the day of the operation the crews went for their main meal before flying and that turned out to be Pilchards. As Sgt Wade was allergic to fish he decided to miss the meal; however, Flt/Lt Machin decided that he would not only have his portion of the Pilchards but that of Sgt Wade as well.

During the outward leg of the operation Flt/Lt Machin was taken very ill while at the controls and unable to continue to fly the aircraft. Sgt Wade had, in the past, made a point of asking pilots for some instruction in flying the aircraft - just in case a pilot became incapacitated, for whatever reason; he left his post in the rear turret and made his way to the cockpit. Once at the controls he brought the aircraft, which by now had dropped from 20,000 feet to 12,000 feet, back under full control. Deciding that they could not now continue with the mission Sgt Wade put the aircraft into a wide and gentle turn. At the end of this manoeuvre he was informed by the navigator that they were not heading for home; his turn had taken them through 360^0 and they were still on track for the target!

A second attempt proved more successful, but this time Sgt Wade was informed by the navigator that his turn had been so wide it had taken them over the most heavily defended island in the area, yet not a shot was fired at them. Mr. Wade told me that the navigator was of the opinion that

TAKING THE WINGS OF THE MORNING

the Germans obviously thought, from the way the aircraft was being flown, they had problems enough and did not pose a threat.

Another new face in the crew, that month, was P/O Finucane who joined as the wireless operator. P/O Finucane was the brother of "Paddy" Finucane, the fighter ace, and stayed for just four sorties.

On 30th and 31st of the month there were two exciting events for the squadron. On 30th they were visited by H. R. H. The Duke of Kent and Air Vice Marshall J. E. A. Baldwin CB. CBE. DSO. AFC; on 31st " A JU88 flying low over the airfield in the early hours of the morning was shot down - wrecked and the four crew killed". The ORB does not say which event gave the squadron more satisfaction.

August brought an increase in operational sorties for Ian, with seven operations being flown to seven different target areas; Essen, Duisberg, Osnabruck, a mine laying operation off Juist, Emden, Kassel and Nuremburg.

An operation planned for 2 August was cancelled late in the evening, due to bad weather conditions. This was the fourth operation that Ian and his crew had had cancelled on them. One cannot begin to understand the extra stress and strain that these cancellations must have put on the aircrews. Having found that they were to fly that night the tension, nerves and fear would have mounted throughout the day; to then have the mission cancelled, sometimes when they were already on board awaiting instructions for take-off, must have caused intolerable strain. Ian had four further operations cancelled this month because of general bad weather or fog. The last to be cancelled in August was on 31st; the target should have been Stuttgart.

The second operation, on 6 August, saw the coming together of what was to be a regular crew, until some changes in the middle of September, flying a total of 14 operations together. Since 21 July, Sgt Mullen had been Ian's regular navigator and now they were joined by Sgt Sauve (Wireless Operator), Sgt Springer (Front Gunner) and Sgt Martin (Rear Gunner). This operation was the last in a series of five raids on Duisberg taken over a period of three weeks. Little real industrial damage had been caused, with a cost to the RAF of 43 aircraft lost.

On 9 August there was a raid on Osnabruck with eight aircraft of 101 Squadron detailed to take part. The ORB states that three aircraft encountered enemy fighters but evaded them; it does not, unfortunately, specify which of the aircraft were involved.

TAKING THE WINGS OF THE MORNING

The mining operation was carried out on 13th of the month with 10 aircraft being detailed. The notes for Ian's aircraft show that two vegetables (mines) were planted (dropped into position) at 01:02 hrs from a height of 700 feet. Three out of the ten aircraft were unsuccessful through bad weather and the failure of navigational equipment.

The Squadron relocated to another airfield, Stradishall, on the same day.

A daylight raid on North German Ports was planned for, and launched on, 21 August. Only two out of the six aircraft detailed for this attack managed to bomb their allotted targets; due to failing cloud cover two aircraft were recalled and the last two encountered similar conditions and turned back. For Ian and his crew, who returned early due to the failure of the cloud cover, the furthest point they reached was $52^0.23'$ N and $05°.10'$ E, an area just North-east of Amsterdam. They jettisoned two 500lb bombs and brought back six 500lb bombs.

On 25th the records show that Ian was operating as a "taxi" service; "F/L Menzies picked up W/O Ollier and crew at Bradwell Bay and ferried them to Martlesham Heath where W/O Ollier ferried "R" back to base".

TAKING THE WINGS OF THE MORNING

Kassel was the target for the raid on 27 August. For the first time Ian was to have a second pilot, or Captain u/t as it is shown in the Battle Orders. Presumably the u/t stands for "under training". Ian and his crew dropped their bomb load, 810 x 4lb incendiary bombs, from 11,000 feet at 23:40. They had used a visual pinpoint for the drop, a Sugar Loaf part of the river to the East of the town. Ian reports that the bombs were seen to explode in the West of the town. Reports from Kassel state that one hundred and forty-four building were destroyed, and a further three hundred and seventeen severely damaged after this attack by three hundred and six aircraft. The RAF paid a high price for this raid with 10.1% of the force being lost. 101 Squadron received a share of the losses with one aircraft crash-landing at Martlesham and burning out. This aircraft had been hit twice by flak on its way back, the W/T operator being slightly injured. Also, night fighters attacked it and the rear gunner was wounded. A second Wellington from 101 Squadron came down in the sea and three of the five crew were rescued by HMS Attentif. A third Wellington, captained by Sgt Beale, failed to return.

September 1942 was to be Ian's last, and busiest, month with 101 Squadron before being moved onto more restful duties as his tour expired. On 1st, nine aircraft of the squadron participated in a raid on Saarbrucken; all returning safely. Ian's report says that they bombed from 15,000 feet at

02:09, with the built-up areas clearly seen and bombs observed to burst in the town. The town appeared to be ablaze with the fires being seen, from seventy miles away, on their return.

However, looking at the ground reports, again taken from Bomber Command War Diaries by Martin Middlebrook & Chris Everitt, it seems that this "success" was not all that it was thought to be. Two hundred and five aircraft claimed good bombing results but the problem was that it was not Saarbrucken that was bombed. Some 13 miles North-west of Saarbrucken, is Saarlouis, which is situated in a similar bend in the river Saar as Saarbrucken. The report goes on to state that the community of Saarlouis was "enraged" to be bombed so heavily. Saarbrucken escaped unscathed.

Operating again on the next night, 2 September, Ian and his, by now, usual crew of Sergeants Springer, Sauve, Mullen and Martin took part in a raid on Karlsruhe. Once again the bomb load, dropped from 18,000 feet, consisted of a total of 3,200lb of incendiary bombs.

A rest of one night followed and then they were back to operational flying, this time to Bremen. On this raid the Pathfinder force tried a new method of marking the target area. This consisted of a three wave attack. The first part of the force would drop white flares to light up the general target area, a second section of the Pathfinder force would, if they identified the aiming points, drop coloured flares and the third and final wave would then drop their load, of all incendiary bombs, on the coloured flares. The entry against Ian's aircraft in the ORB records states that their incendiary bombs were released and seen to ignite on target.

Serious damage was done to the Weser aircraft works and the Atlas shipyard. A strain must have been put on the German glass production as ground reports say that on top of four hundred and sixty houses being destroyed a further six thousand had their windows broken in this raid.

An entry in the station diary for 6 September is headed "Congratulatory message" and is followed by "At 10.16 hrs. The AOC No. 3 Group broadcast a message to all the crews who took part in the raid on Bremen on the night of the 4/5 of September". A pat on the back from the command but there was no let up in the pressure, as that night it was off to Duisberg again for Ian and his crew. The entry in the ORB for this night shows that with his rank of Flt/Lt Ian would have been the senior pilot and therefore, presumably, leading the squadron on this raid. 101 Squadron lost one of the eight aircraft that were dispatched on this raid; Flt/Sgt Williams and his crew did not return and nothing was heard from his aircraft.

TAKING THE WINGS OF THE MORNING

The next night, 7 September, had seven aircraft of 101 Squadron detailed for a raid on Warnemunde, to bomb the Heinkel works. Ian's aircraft, still X3457, was again loaded with incendiaries and, also this time, a camera. All aircraft were recalled after take-off, no reason being shown in the records. Again one wonders whether this news would have come as a welcome relief as they were heading back home to safety or would it have been viewed with some distress as it meant that they would have to go through all the preparations, hopes and fears, again, maybe the next night. Ian and his crew had two further operation cancelled this month.

The squadron was operational again on the following night, with Ian and his crew leading the nine aircraft dispatched from the Squadron. The Pathfinder force had difficulty in locating the target, Frankfurt, and it seems that most of the bombing fell on a town 15 miles to the South-west. Three Wellingtons of 101 Squadron were forced to return early because of engine troubles, but those that completed the raid reported that huge fires could be seen from as far away as 90 miles.

With no let up in demand for their services Ian and his crew were operational again the following night, making seven operations in just nine nights. This time it was Gardening (mine laying) off Heligoland. Eight aircraft from 101 Squadron, all carrying two 1,500lb mines, and led by

Squadron Leader Patterson, laid their mines successfully and returned safely.

After a short break from operations, just three nights, the crew of X3457, Ian and his four sergeants, took off on Sunday 13 September, to join a large force attacking Bremen. They hit the Lloyd dynamo works and part of the Focke-Wolfe factory. This was the last time that the five of them were to fly together as a complete crew, Sergeants Mullen and Martin being posted out. It was also the last time that Ian was to pilot X3457 on an operation.

On Monday 14 September, 101 Squadron participated in a raid on Wilhelmshaven. Ian, with two new crew members (P/O Derry replacing Sgt Mullen and Sgt Franchuck replacing Sgt Springer), flying Wellington X3812 carrying 3,200lbs of incendiaries, bombed at 22:40 from 16,000 feet. Port Haven was pinpointed by the light from the Pathfinders' flares but Ian was " Unable to identify own bomb bursts among so many". Two hundred and two aircraft took part in the raid with the loss of only two Wellingtons. All 101 Squadron aircraft returned safely.

Ian had one night off, but was then back to operations on 16 September. Again a different aircraft and another change in the crew, Sgt Suave being replaced by Sgt Gould. Takeoff was at 20:25 that evening to form up with another 11 aircraft from the squadron. This group then joined other squadrons to build a raiding force of 369 aircraft. The bombing on this raid, on Essen, was scattered with many other towns being hit. From the notes entered alongside Ian's aircraft in the ORB I assume that the wide area of bombing was due to poor visibility. The entry states that bombing was carried out by a combination of bearing (160^0) and the ETA over target plus flares and fires. However, the entry in the Bomber Command War Diaries states "Although much of the bombing was scattered, this was probably the most successful attack on this difficult target"; the entry in the diaries continues to detail the damage to Essen and the surrounding towns. This did, however, prove to be a costly raid to the RAF with 39 aircraft being lost, including one from 101 Squadron. Ian's next two sorties, scheduled for 18 & 19 September were cancelled.

Saturday 26 September 1942 was the day that Ian flew his last mission with 101 Squadron. With yet another crew change, Sgt Gould being replaced by Sgt Nichols, Ian took-off on another mine-laying operation in the "Western Baltic Area". The squadron diary for this day has an entry which states that " A recall message because of bad weather was sent to the aircraft by Headquarters No 3 Group. The aircraft were instructed to jettison their mines before returning, but four of the Wellingtons did not receive the message and proceeded with their mission. The crews of these aircraft claimed to have laid their mines in the allotted positions, and parachutes and splashes were observed. All aircraft returned safely to base".

Ian and his crew were one of the four that did not receive the recall message; the notes in the ORB, alongside Ian's aircraft state "2 vegetables (mines) planted at 00:50 at 10 sec. Intervals from 900 feet. 2 Parachutes seen on a heading of 045°".

This was the end of Ian's "Tour" and he was posted out to take on other duties. A "Tour" was normally 30 operations but I have only been able to find Ian involved with twenty nine during his time with 101 Squadron. Maybe he had completed the missing operation when he was with the Operational Training Unit or, perhaps, it was just a case of his skills being needed elsewhere.

While with the squadron he had been recommended for an award and on 6 November 1942 the following notice appeared in the London Gazette.

Distinguished Flying Cross

Acting Flight Lieutenant John Watherstone Menzies (108868) RAFVR No 101 Squadron

This officer has displayed outstanding coolness and courage under all circumstances. Throughout the time he has served in this squadron, Flight Lieutenant Menzies has been responsible for promoting a very high standard of keenness and efficiency. He has proved himself fully competent to command his flight in the absence of a Commander.

TAKING THE WINGS OF THE MORNING

The notice of the award prompted an immediate response from his old squadron, now based at Holme - on - Spalding - Moor. One can only guess at what the marking of the occasion in "the approved" style meant!

> Royal Air Force Station,
> Holme-on-Spalding-Moor,
> Yorks.
>
> 101B/C/726/4/P.1.   7th November, 1942.
>
> Dear Menzies,
>
> The entire Squadron join me in heartiest congratulations on your award of the D.F.C.
>
> We are only sorry that you cannot be with us to mark the occasion in the approved style.
>
> With all Good Wishes.
>
> Yours sincerely,
>
> Wing Commander, Commanding,
> No. 101 Squadron, R.A.F.
>
> P/Lt. J.W. Menzies, D.F.C.
> Officers Mess,
> 1483 T.T. & G. Flight,
> R.A.F. Station,
> MARHAM.

TAKING THE WINGS OF THE MORNING

It was to take a further three months before the official invitation to receive the award from King George at Buckingham Palace arrived. On 16 February Ian, accompanied by his proud mother and one of his sisters, no doubt equally proud, received his award from the King.

TAKING THE WINGS OF THE MORNING

CENTRAL CHANCERY OF
THE ORDERS OF KNIGHTHOOD,
ST JAMES'S PALACE, S.W.1.

4th February, 1943.

CONFIDENTIAL.

Sir,

    The King will hold an Investiture at Buckingham Palace on Tuesday, the 16th February, 1943, at which your attendance is requested.

    It is requested that you should be at the Palace not later than 10.15 o'clock a.m.

    DRESS—Service Dress, Morning Dress or Civil Defence Uniform.

    This letter should be produced on entering the Palace, as no further card of admission will be issued.

    Two tickets for relations or friends to witness the Investiture may be obtained on application to this Office and you are requested to state your requirements on the form enclosed.

    Please complete the enclosed form and <u>return immediately</u> to the Secretary, Central Chancery of the Orders of Knighthood, St. James's Palace, London, S.W.1.

        I am, Sir,

            Your obedient Servant,

Flight Lieutenant John W. Menzies,
    D.F.C., R.A.F.V.R.

                        Secretary.

TAKING THE WINGS OF THE MORNING

Having related Ian's flying career with 101 Squadron perhaps now is the time, as I could not find a way of doing it in the main text, to make special mention of the unsung heroes of the RAF; the Ground Crews. Without these dedicated people, who had to work on the aircraft, often in terrible condition of cold, wind and rain, out on the airfield, the crews of the aircraft could not have carried the war to Germany. I believe a special bond was formed between the air and ground crews and it is also my belief that the ground crews have not been given the recognition they so richly deserve. I hope that in some way these few words may do something to redress the balance and make people remember those behind the scenes.

THE MIDDLE PERIOD

SEPTEMBER 1942
-
MARCH 1944

TAKING THE WINGS OF THE MORNING

In many ways this period of Ian's service with the RAF is the hardest to write about because of the lack of detailed information available.

Having left 101 Squadron at the end of his "tour", Ian was posted to 1483 Target Towing & Gunnery Flight, based at Marham, on flying duties. However, he was only here for a few days before being transferred to 1657 HCU (Heavy Conversion Unit) as an instructor.

It is odd that he should be posted as an instructor as 1657, based at Stradishall, were operating four engined Stirling aircraft. Ian's time as a pilot had been spent on the twin engined Wellington. Perhaps this is why the next entry on his record shows a move back to Marham and 1483 (Bomber) Gunner Flight only one week after being posted to 1657 HCU.

The next entry on Ian's record shows a move, just four days later, back to 1483 Target Towing and Gunnery Flight. Why there should be this change after only four days I have been unable to discover.

Ian was now to stay with 1483 TT&G for 17 months with just one week taken out in November 1942 where the entry shows that he was on a

53

"Course at Civilian Technical Corps". Where this course was and the content of the course I have been unable to discover.

One of Ian's duties while on 1483 TT&G was to pilot the aircraft that was used to tow the target which the gunners, both airborne and ground based, used for training/practice. The piloting of this aircraft involved putting the machine through, often violent, manoeuvres that caused the target to take on the attitude of an actual aircraft.

Ian's sister, Mona, has told me that when he was involved with these duties the motion of the aircraft made him feel extremely ill. The only food he could, often for days on end, eat was plain bread and butter!

There are very few entries in 1483's record book that actually mention individuals by name which makes this part of Ian's story so thin as far as information is concerned. However, among the few names that are mentioned one is of the individual who was to go on to be Ian's navigator on 161 Sqdn; F/O K R Bunney. Between 5 May 1942 and the time he left 1483 TT&G to join 161 Sqdn F/O Bunney flew, as navigator, on several air-sea rescue missions. Two other names that appear within these records and later turn up in 161 Squadron's records are those of Helfer and Hale

Ian's name appears for the first time on 13 November 1943 when he was one of three pilots, flying Martinets, involved in an air-sea rescue search for a "bailed-out air crew". There is no mention as to whether or not the search was successful. This was followed by two further rescue flights, one on 23 November 1943 and a second on 28 January 1944; again there was no result recorded.

After this last mention there is no further trace of Ian until 15 March 1944 when he is noted in 161 Squadron's records as being posted in from 1483 TT&G.

In March 1944 1483 TT&G was disbanded and Ian transferred to 161 Squadron based at Tempsford.

MORE INFORMATION

&

THE FINDING AND RECOVERY

OF

FK790

JULY 1997

TAKING THE WINGS OF THE MORNING

The hunt for information regarding Ian's time with 161 Squadron has proved not only extremely difficult, but has taken many years. The process of gathering information has put me in touch with many fascinating and interesting people in several different countries; creating a complicated web with many leads and sources interacting with one another.

For ease of telling and to avoid some of the complexities of the web that has been spun I will try to relate the events that provided me with so much information in a manner that is as untangled as possible. Therefore some of the events and meetings may not be in strict chronological order.

Somewhere along the way, after my meeting at Tangmere and my first bumbling efforts to find more about this part of Ian's career, I had been given a "reading list" of books that covered the work of the Secret Squadrons. It was while reading one of these books I came across a reference to Ian, his crew and agents having been lost on a mission to Holland on 5/6 July 1944. So now I had another two pieces in the puzzle, the date and a place, albeit it a very big place at this stage.

My next major breakthrough came in 1990 when, once again sorting through some of the papers I had inherited, I came across a press cutting from 1945. This told part of the story of Tempsford airfield and mentioned one pub and one hotel where the aircrews would gather when not on duty. From directory enquiries I obtained the numbers of both of these establishments and thought I would try a very long shot and see if they could add any information about the Squadrons that had operated from Tempsford and the air and ground crew who would have been their patrons all those years ago. The first one I rang was the Anchor hotel. This was to prove to be the most important step I was to make in my search as it opened the door for all that has followed since.

When I rang the hotel in the vague hope they could possibly tell me something of the events in the area in 1944 the answer exceeded all my hopes. I could never have imagined that I was just about to "hit the jackpot". I was informed that the veterans of both of the Secret Squadrons, relatives and some of the agents that passed through Tempsford were soon to have their annual reunion there. The hotel also gave me the telephone number of the organiser of the event.

It was with some trepidation and yet with a heart full of high hopes that I rang the organiser with the intention of asking if I might be allowed to come to the gathering and talk to the people there in the hope of meeting someone who would remember Ian. The idea was to explain the reason behind my quest and what information I had gathered; unfortunately I got a very cool reception. In fact, I was almost totally discouraged from pursuing the matter further.

However I decided, rightly or wrongly, to go along to the hotel anyway and, hopefully, make contact with someone who was willing to help. When Helen and I arrived at the hotel we asked if someone could point out the organiser of the reunion, I went over to introduce myself and once again was given a very cool reception. Unfortunately, during the time in the hotel, before their lunch, no opportunity presented itself to allow us to get to talk to anyone. Both Helen and I were acutely aware that we were very much outsiders; onlookers who felt extremely privileged to be in the company of these men and women.

Helen and I stayed in the bar wondering just what to do next; we had arrived here with such high hopes and now it just appeared to have been a wasted journey. Yet fortune was on our side after all.

Seated at the bar was a gentleman who was looking through a catalogue of medals; soon we got talking and he turned out to be very helpful. His name was Norman Didwell and his interest in the squadron was to do with one of the ex Squadron Commanders, W/C Pickard. Having explained to Norman what I was attempting to do he gave me an address of a Dutch historian/researcher who might possibly be able to help. This, too, was a major breakthrough in my search.

While the people at the reunion had been having their lunch I had noticed that one of the attendees was Sir Alan Boxer, Ian's commanding officer in 1944. I decided that somehow I would have to get to talk to him. Helen and I waited outside the hotel for the party to emerge and to go on their way to the "Barn", on the airfield, for the service that was to be held there.

My chance soon came and I approached the gentleman I recognised as Sir Alan, with a file containing all I knew about Ian's career, and a reasonable 10in x 8in portrait of Ian in his uniform. For anyone watching it must of looked like a very poor impression of "This is your Life" as I approached, then introduced myself, clutching my file of notes and pictures, to Sir Alan. Once again I was met with a very cold reception and was told bluntly that, when shown a picture of Ian, he did not remember him. With the benefit of hindsight I now realise that I had made the totally wrong approach; I also heard later that some people who were there thought I was from the press. It was almost as though it was a case of "secret then and still secret now".

TAKING THE WINGS OF THE MORNING

Despite getting no further information Helen and I followed the group to the Barn on the airfield for the service; this was perhaps one of the most moving events I have experienced. At the end of the service we left the airfield and headed for home with the feeling of nothing achieved; in fact, if anything, some damage was done and the possibility of future contacts jeopardised.

Once home we reviewed the situation and decided to follow up the lead that Norman had given us. I wrote to his contact, Aad Neeven, in Holland, and then we could do no more than wait to see what transpired. After a short while I received a letter bearing a post mark showing that it originated from the far East. It was from Aad who was working overseas and had had my enquiry forwarded to him. Aad very quickly managed to throw much more light on the subject of Ian and his mission.

It appears that during all the time I had spent in the Public Record Office at Kew, sometimes trying to access files that I found to be still closed under the 50 year rule, there was a book available, off the shelf, in Holland that contained much of the information I was searching for. In 1991 Aad sent me a letter in which contained a translation of passages from this book which was entitled, "They Jumped by Moonlight" by Eddie De Roever. Along with the information on the agents and their efforts to get to England there was also a photocopy of a page from the book that had a map on it showing the area of the crash site in the IJselmeer.

Now things really appeared to be moving swiftly; some five years after the start of my search, I now knew what that last mission had been named, the names of the agents and the area where the aircraft had crashed. The possession of this information caused me to alter my objectives. Surely now that the area of the crash had been identified it might be possible to find Ian's remains.

I knew that Ian had no known grave, as his name was on one of the panels at the Air Forces Memorial at Runnymede. I assumed that his body must be in a Commonwealth War Grave which probably had the inscription "An Unknown Airman" on the headstone. It seemed to me that all I had to do was to work out where Ian's body could have been washed ashore, find a nearby cemetery that had a grave of an "unknown Airman" in it and then Ian was found. Oh! The joy of blissful ignorance.

Over the next two or three years I checked, through the Commonwealth War Graves Commission, the areas that seemed possible and the cemeteries within those areas that contained graves of unknown airmen. What had seemed such a simple idea was to turn out to be a much bigger task than I had thought. After several conversations with the staff at the CWGC I got the impression that if I could identify a cemetery and the grave I thought to be Ian's and supply reasonable proof that the remains buried there were his then they would try to confirm the identity. It seemed to me that I had to prove that the remains were his and then they would try to prove the identity. It all seemed a bit strange to me and very frustrating.

I tried all the ways I could think of to narrow down the numbers of possible cemeteries: I checked tide tables, with the help of the British Royal Navy, and currents to see if it was possible that his body might have been washed through the sluice gates from the IJsselmeer and into the Waddenzee. If this had been the case there was a chance that his body could have come ashore on one of the Friesian Islands.

The task prove to be much more complicated than I had expected and, eventually, the CWGC wrote to me and explained, very politely but firmly, that they could not spend any more time on this case but wished me well with my efforts in the future.

TAKING THE WINGS OF THE MORNING

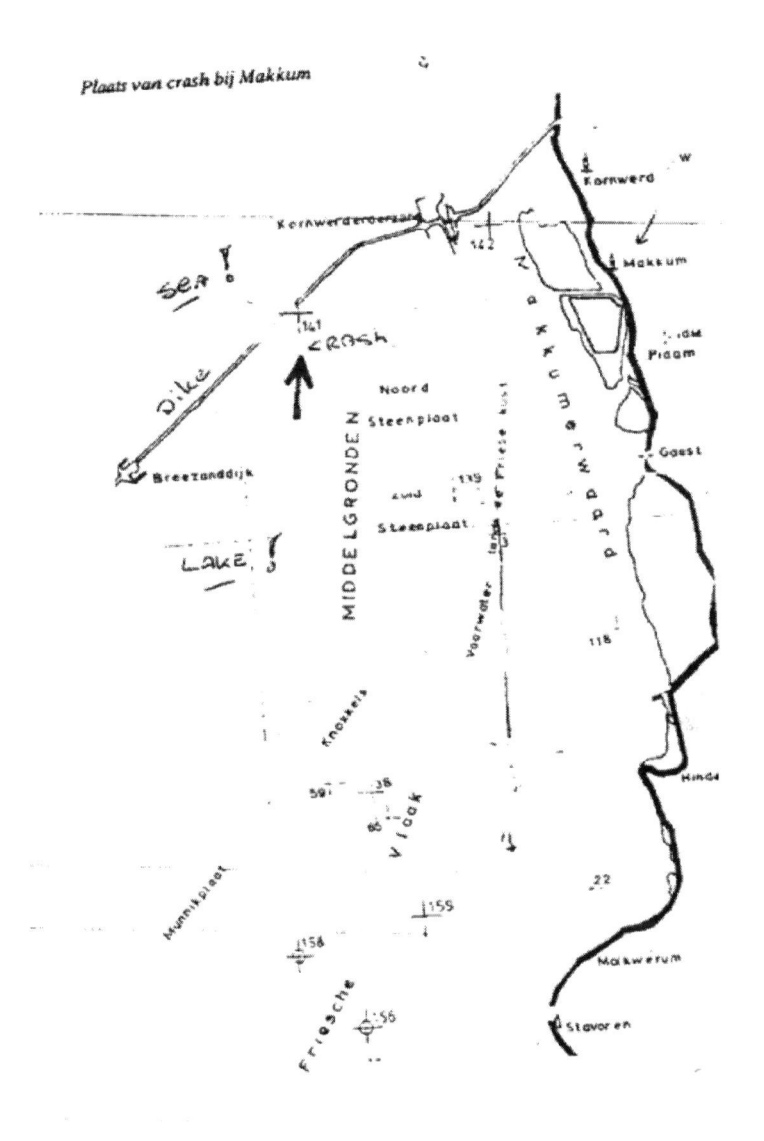

Plan of the crash site

TAKING THE WINGS OF THE MORNING

I decided to abandon this approach and to continue searching records at Kew, to read all the books that had been on my "reading list" and also to keep up my correspondence with Aad.

Over the next couple of years I tended to let the matter rest. From time to time I would get a phone call or a letter which would revive my flagging enthusiasm. In general, however, my efforts to make further progress became half-hearted and spasmodic, the visits to Kew few and far between.

I tried to contact some of the authors of the books I had read in the hope that they may have had some information that they had not put into their books but to no avail.

One lead I did receive, although now I cannot remember where it came from, was that one of the Lysander pilots, Leslie Montgomery, had had his story published in a South African newspaper some years back. I managed to contact the correct paper and they were kind enough to search back many years through their archives to find the story. The story had been stored on microfilm and they said they would print a copy off and send it to me. Once again I experienced a rush of adrenaline; the chase was on again.

TAKING THE WINGS OF THE MORNING

In due course a package arrived from South Africa and , with great excitement, I opened it. Inside, with several sheets of prints from microfilm, was a short letter apologising for the standard of the copies. From the look of the first page it certainly looked clear and readable but with each successive page the quality dramatically reduced until, after only two or three pages, the text was unreadable. Once again the feeling of exhilaration was dashed and replaced by disappointment and frustration. The next major breakthrough was not to come until early 1994. It really did seem that I had exhausted all possible avenues of enquiry.

At the beginning of 1994 I found a letter from Aad which contained the name and address of a researcher in England, a Mr. Ernest Hardy. I wrote to him, explaining how I had obtained his name, giving him as much detail as I could in a short letter and then waited to see what would transpire.

In the middle of March 1994 I received a reply from Mr. Hardy saying that he had written to the widow of Sgt Withers, now Mrs. Pearson, who was also looking for information regarding the last flight of FK790.

At the end of the month I received a letter from Mrs. Pearson saying that she had been contacted by Mr. Hardy and unfortunately she did not think she could add anything to the information already in my possession.

However, she was kind enough to send me photocopies of the pages from Sgt Withers' log book for the time he was flying with Ian.

Very soon a strong bond was formed and regular correspondence began, over the next few years I kept Mrs. Pearson (Joan) informed of any new snippet of information that came in.

By now Helen and I had started to make good progress in our search at the Public Records Office, Kew. Much of the information we were seeking was now being revealed to us, although some files were still closed to the public. Soon we had copies of 161 squadron's Operational Record Book covering the period of Ian's service with them. This allowed us to identify all the missions flown by Ian and his crew. However the ORB only gave us the basic information and statistics. Luckily it was not long before we discovered the file that contained the pilots' debriefing notes and, sure enough, Ian's were there for us to see. I cannot describe the range of emotions I experienced the day that I held some of those documents, signed by Ian half a century earlier. At last I had the proof of the nature of his work during those months at Tempsford. Details that Ian could not relay to anyone at the time and which had, therefore, remained secret for 50 years. Yet again I was charged with enthusiasm; another piece fitted nicely into the jigsaw. Now the puzzle was complete and that is how it was to stay for many months. Once again leads and information dried up, all progress was halted and hopes dashed.

Now I spent what time I did devote to my research trying to consolidate the information I had rather than break new ground. Joan and I talked many times during this period and I am so glad that we did. On Monday 21 July 1997, around lunchtime, I had a call from Joan with the most wonderful, yet shattering, news. The first question she asked was "Had I heard the news?". When I asked her what she meant by this she replied "They've found the wreck of Ian's aircraft and are in the process of raising it from the seabed in Holland, and there are human remains in the cockpit". I do not think I have ever had such a shock before or since. I was speechless, unable to say a word for fear of breaking down such was the rush of emotions. When I had recovered my composure I managed to ask Joan some sensible questions and when I gave her a chance to reply Joan supplied some answers.

She had had a phone call that morning from a gentleman she knew in Holland. A man she had met one year when she took part in the Dutch remembrance ceremony that is held at the beginning of May each year, named Klaas Groeneveld.

TAKING THE WINGS OF THE MORNING

Joan gave me his phone number and I rang him, without delay, not knowing what to expect or even say. When I got through to him I explained, perhaps in a garbled way, who I was and the nature of my connection with the aircraft that had been found. Luckily, it seemed that Joan had already explained, at least in part, who I was and therefore Klaas could make sense of my confused and rushed explanations. I told Klaas that if I could get leave from my company I intended to get the first available flight to Holland. Should this be so, I asked if he could tell me how to get to Makkum and book me a hotel room in the town. Without hesitation Klaas told me not to worry about trying to get to Makkum by public transport as he would pick me up from the airport and, also, not to be concerned about accommodation as I would be staying with him.

I was granted leave by the company and booked myself on the first available flight from Luton to Amsterdam and hastily made several phone calls to let others know the fantastic news I had received. Without thinking of the implications of international time zones I rang my aunt Mona, Ian's sister, in Australia. It was three o'clock in the morning, local time, when I was connected to her number. I still clearly remember the conversation. I just blurted out "We've found Ian!", to which she replied, giving proof to my theory that she still hoped that he might not have been killed, "Is he alive?". I then had to explain just want had transpired in the last few hours and informed her I would be in touch again just as soon as I knew more. The fact that Mona took this bombshell totally in her stride, far more calmly than I had, says a great deal for the strength of her character; something she was to demonstrate again later. My brother, Rick, reacted in much the same way as I had when I rang him at work. There was just a stunned silence, followed by some questions delivered in a very weak and trembling voice. Again I had to say that I would pass on an update as soon as I knew more. During these few hours before I left for Luton Helen did a wonderful job of calming me down, (the surge of adrenaline and emotions had been enormous), and generally getting me organised.

On my arrival at Schiphol airport I was immensely relieved to see a man holding a card with my name on it. This was my first meeting with Klaas, a man who, along with his family, had without any hesitation reached out to help a stranger. This was my first experience of Dutch hospitality and kindness. Without delay we left the airport and headed north-east towards Makkum. During the journey Klaas briefed me on how the wreckage had been found and what had been happening during the course of the last few days.

Klaas explained that a local research group had been looking for an aircraft that had crashed in the area during 1944 but did not have the exact location and, despite the specialist equipment they had at their disposal, had been unable to locate the wreck. However, local fisherman Jan Bootsma remembered a story told to him by his father Fimme Bootsma, the fisherman who found the body of Jan Bockma, one of the four Dutch agents onboard the aircraft. The information given to him by his father allowed Jan to lead the expedition to an area where, in the past, fishermen had got their nets caught. On Saturday 5 July 1997 the diving and research group was on board Jan's boat and by using the magnetometer and radar they were able to establish that there was a wreck of an aircraft on the sea bed. By coincidence, the day the wreckage was located was 53 years, to the day, after Hudson FK790 fell from the sky to remain hidden despite an attempt to recover the aircraft in 1945. Very quickly a dive was organised and a few small parts of the wreckage brought to the surface. It was soon established that the wreck still held quantities of both ammunition and explosives; because of the position of the wreck relative to the vitally important locks between the IJsselmeer and the Waddenzee and its proximity to the shipping lane a decision was made to raise the wreck. Normally it would have been left undisturbed as a war grave. Various groups and organisations were brought together and the salvage operation planned and started.

TAKING THE WINGS OF THE MORNING

As we crossed the causeway that separates the IJselmeer from the Waddenzee Klaas said that he hoped we would be able to meet Jan Bootsma and be taken on board his boat out to the recovery vessels. Yet once again I was to be disappointed; by the time we arrived at the spot where Klaas expected to meet Jan the berth was empty. Jan had already sailed and from where Klaas and I stood we could see that the salvage vessels were first preparing and then leaving the site for a port to offload the wreckage.

We proceeded to Makkum and Klaas' house where I was made most welcome and shown to a room from which his son had been "evicted" to make room for me. By this time I was feeling extremely tired and emotionally exhausted, for within twenty-four hours I had received the news from Joan Pearson, had a reporter from a daily news paper arrive on my doorstep at around midnight, travelled to Luton and flown to Holland to be met by Klaas and now was wondering just what to do or what was to happen next

Klaas gave me directions to the churchyard where the crew was buried and, having explained my need to have some time to myself, left to visit the cemetery and see where the events of the 5/6 July 1944 had finished for three of the four crew. When, after a short time spent in quiet contemplation, I returned to Klaas' house I found that he had another visitor. I was introduced to the lady who had arrived; my first meeting with Annie Bockma, the sister of Jan Bockma. What followed the introductions is still a bit of a blur, I do, however, remember that once again I experienced a whole range of emotions as information was exchanged and gaps in both our information filled. This was the first of many meetings and laid the foundation for a lasting friendship. Klaas had being doing some detective work and found that the wreckage was to be brought ashore, at the port of Sneek, the next morning, and so an early start was required as he was going to drive me to the port before returning me to Schiphol airport.

We arrived at the quay side in Sneek just as the crew of the salvage vessel were preparing to off load the last of the wreckage onto a convoy of lorries; once again luck was on my side. Klaas found the master of the salvage vessel and explained who I was and why we were there. Without any hesitation I was invited on board the barge that carried the bent and twisted metal that had once been my uncle's aircraft. Klaas, acting as interpreter, told me I was free to look around the wreckage by myself and in my own time. Scattered on deck there were large pieces, small pieces, pieces that were immediately recognisable and others that were distorted beyond recognition.

TAKING THE WINGS OF THE MORNING

There were three large pieces that stood out from the rest and were easily identified; one of the engines, a bent and barnacle encrusted propeller and a sizeable piece of the tail section and fuselage. On close inspection it was possible to make out, still relatively clearly, even after fifty-three years below the surface, the legend FK790. So, here before me, was a sight I had never dreamed I would see. The flood of emotions I experienced when I gently and falteringly traced the letters and numbers on that piece of metal ranged from great sadness to great joy, relief and disbelief; I was awed, humbled and once again rendered speechless. The lump in my throat felt as though it would surely choke me. Trying to take photographs was made difficult by the amount of moisture that had suddenly formed in my eyes making focusing nigh on impossible.

I accepted the invitation of the vessel's master, Mr. Waggenmakker, to take some of the smaller items from the boxes that stretched out along the deck and contained many, many pieces of wreckage. There were pieces of what looked like radio equipment, a piece of material that I was told was a parachute, fragments of Perspex that had come from the cockpit or gunner's turret and many items whose function I could not determine. Before long the offloading had been completed and there was nothing left for me to see, much less do, so Klaas and I left for Schiphol. I was exhausted, emotionally drained and yet, somehow, felt as though a great weight had been lifted and my heart was singing.

Now everything seemed so simple; I had seen the aircraft registration lettering with my own eyes, it was certainly the aircraft Ian had taken-off in all those years ago and human remains had been found in the cockpit. Therefore the answer was perfectly clear; Ian had been found.

Once back in England I again contacted RAF Insworth (Casualty) and informed them that, following my correspondence of some years earlier, my uncle had now been found. The staff there were extremely kind and helpful and we agreed that I should go down and meet them as perhaps I could supply some of the missing information. When we met they told me that this case was rather different to the others they handled. Normally, they said, when a missing airman was found it was they who had the task, often long and complicated, of tracing any living relatives. In this case the relative had come to tell them the remains had been found. A complete reversal!

At the end of a very pleasant meeting they gave me a warning that things were not as simple as they seemed to me. Just because remains had been found in the cockpit of the correct aircraft, it did not necessarily mean that they were Ian's. I was informed that now a positive identification had to be made and that this might take some time. I must confess that I was both surprised and disappointed by this news, I resigned myself to waiting and yet still trying to proceed with my research.

I think it was around a month after returning from Holland that I received a call from Annie Bockma inviting Helen and me to go to visit her as she had some things to show us and would like a meeting with us that was, perhaps, more private than the time we had met at Klaas' house. Delighted to receive the invitation Helen and I arranged a flight to Schiphol, this time to be met by Annie. On the journey from the airport to her house we stopped off at a museum that she wanted us to see, the Kazamatten Museum at Kornwerdezand, which housed an exhibition dedicated to the resistance movement that had been in the area. Here another happy coincidence took place. The gentleman who was to be our guide was Cees Scheepvaart, the son of Abele Scheepvaart the Dutch police officer who had played such an important part in the events that followed the crash of the aircraft. This meeting was to give me yet more information regarding the events that followed the recovery of the bodies of the IJselmeer. This information tied in with the autopsy reports that had been given to me by, I believe, Aad Neveen.

TAKING THE WINGS OF THE MORNING

After our visit we went on to Annie's house and here she had a video that had been given to her that she wanted to show us. It had been taken by the salvage team and showed clearly, and in detail, the recovery of the pieces of the wreck and the careful way the mud and slurry were searched to ensure that even the smallest artefact was not missed.

Watching this video really brought home the enormity of the find. I am happy to say that I was able to supply a small present for Annie; she had told me, when we met at Klaas', that she did not have a good picture of her brother Jan. All she had was a small, passport sized, photo of him that she had carried with for all those years and was now badly creased. What she did not know was that Aad Neveen had sent me the negatives of small pictures of the four agents. I had had these copied and was now able to give Annie a large, top quality picture of her beloved brother. Sadly we were only able to stay for the one night and had then to return home.

By now we must have been into September and there still had been no news from Insworth so I contacted them to see what was happening and was told that they had a small problem. They required Ian's dental records from the RAF to make the identification and the small problem was that they had been destroyed. Another minor point was that there were more remains than there should have been, although they would not elaborate on this and I was told to keep this secret. So just what had they found. Was there another person, perhaps unauthorised, on the aircraft? Had another aircraft crashed in the vicinity? It was something that was to puzzle us for some time. I will come to the answer a bit later on. They asked me if I had any information that might help with the identification. Unfortunately the only distinguishing marks I could think of were that he had had his nose broken and his appendix removed, this of course was of no use. There was nothing else to do but to carry on waiting.

While I was waiting I was still in touch with Joan Pearson and Klaas Groeneveld and, of course, Ian's sister Mona in Australia. Klaas, who had been trying to find the contact address he had for Kenneth Bunney's brother came up trumps. Through directory enquiries I obtained the phone number of one Don Bunney and called him. It was not an easy call to make; I did not want to upset anybody but, at the same time I needed information. I need not have worried as the call went very well and Don informed me of the whereabouts of the third brother Derek and his phone number. So now I had contact with the relatives of two of the three crew members and the sister of one of the agents. I was feeling pretty pleased with myself, although really I was only reaping the rewards of others' efforts.

TAKING THE WINGS OF THE MORNING

Fate too was to lend a hand with another strange and remarkable coincidence. On Monday 10 November 1997 the Daily Mail carried the story of the finding of the aircraft and Ian's remains, although his identity had still had not been confirmed. That day a lady in Andover was unable to buy her usual daily paper and by chance bought the Daily Mail. When she read the half page article covering the events in Holland and my efforts to trace all the relatives of those on board one name stood out from all the others, Sgt Eliot. She rang her father, in Bristol, and asked "Wasn't your father in the RAF?". "Yes" came the reply. "Wasn't he a Sergeant?". Again "Yes". "Had he not been killed in 1944?". Once again the answer was affirmative. Then she suggested her father ought to buy a copy of the paper for himself. It was because of this stroke of pure luck that Helen and I were to have lunch, soon after, with Derek Eliot, the son of Ian's air-gunner Eric Eliot, his wife Daphne and daughter Tracy, who had so fortuitously spotted the article. At that meeting in Andover it gave me enormous pleasure to give Derek a part of the gunner's turret that I had managed to bring back from Holland in July. Now another part of the jigsaw was complete.

The article in The Mail also contained a reference to the photograph I mentioned earlier, in "The Second Beginning". They said, wrongly, that the picture had be found on the body in the cockpit and published it with the caption *"War Hero's Secret Love. Shot down RAF pilot kept this picture. But who is she? Asks his nephew"*.

Not only was their story inaccurate, (I suppose their version made a better story), it also triggered some very odd calls from members of the public who claimed that the *Mystery Woman* was their mother. There was, however one lady who contacted me and explained that her mother had been engaged to a pilot and that they had agreed to wait
until he had finished his tour before they got married, but the airman disappeared while on a mission. She explained that her mother had never really talked about the pilot who was her father and that she had been born after he had been killed. When she showed me some pictures if her mother I agreed that there was definitely a likeness between her mother and the picture found in Ian's wallet. Dates and locations also seemed to fit. Sometime later when Mona, Ian's sister, was in the country we went as far as having a DNA check done. Unfortunately the result showed that there was only a twenty five percent chance that Ian could have been this lady's father, a great disappointment to her.

The TEMPSFORD MONTHS

MARCH 1944

JULY 1944

"Set Europe ablaze"

Winston S Churchill

"..find this viper's nest and obliterate it."

Adolf Hitler

TAKING THE WINGS OF THE MORNING

The best way to describe the workings of, and the secrecy that surrounded, the airfield at Tempsford is probably given in an article that appeared in the Evening Standard on 16 June 1945.

"Tempsford (Beds.) kept one of the war's biggest secrets

R.A.F fly-by-nights
Beat Gestapo

From James Stuart : Tempsford, Thursday

Tempsford is just a hamlet in rural Bedfordshire. Its inhabitants mostly work on the land. And none of them knew it, but Tempsford held one of the big secrets of the war.

They knew that down a little side road marked "This road is closed to the public" there was an R.A.F. Station. In the Anchor and the Wheatsheaf they saw the R.A.F. Men. But that was all. They had no idea of the job they were engaged on.

Names of the pilots and crews who did that job cannot yet be revealed except for one. The late Group Captain P. C. Pickard, D.S.O. and two bars, D.F.C., the famous "Target for Tonight" pilot.

TAKING THE WINGS OF THE MORNING

When he left Bomber Command, Pickard commanded one of the two "Special mission" squadrons which the R.A.F. Created as a link with the underground movement in all occupied countries. He was an expert in "pick up" flights.

The R.A.F. began this branch of its work immediately after the collapse of France - with one flight of a bomber squadron of No 3 Group. By March 1942 Tempsford was in operation, and finally two special squadrons were being employed.

From Tempsford they delivered arms, ammunition, radio sets, food and other supplies to all the underground fighters from the Arctic Circle of northern Norway to the Mediterranean shores of southern France.

From big bombers - Whitleys first and then Stirlings and Halifaxes they dropped their parachute containers. Every kind of supply went down from skis and sleighs for the Norwegians to bicycles and bicycle tyres- made in England but carefully camouflaged with French names - to the resisters in Western Europe.

For three years the airfield, built over what had been a large area of marsh, was the air centre of resistance movements of all Europe. Night after night the villagers saw airplanes go off and probably heard them droning back in the small hours. But they never saw the people, men and women in civilian clothes, who were driven down the prohibited road from the airfield, the men and women who had been brought from Occupied France under the very noses of the Wehrmacht and Gestapo.

NO SECRET DEVICES

There were no secret devices to help this passenger service to operate. The R.A.F. airplanes simply landed in France, picked up their passengers and flew off again to Tempsford.

On other trips they dropped Czech, Polish and Dutch agents in their own countries.

About 700 resistance leaders made the trip. Sometimes the R.A.F. Brought back documents, maps and messages.

Not all the story can be told even now. There is still the need for secrecy about how the great organisation was built up.

The romantic-and a hazardous-side of the job was flying the old unarmed Lysanders and the bigger Hudsons to the secret landing grounds in France guided only by the dim lights from torches held by patriots. All the pick-ups were made in France.

TAKING THE WINGS OF THE MORNING

One of the airmen who took part in the adventure said to-day: "We had to have decent fields so we brought back men of the resistance to teach them the sort of places to select and what to do to help us land. Then we took them back again. Others we brought back were trained in England as saboteurs and dropped again in France."

"WE HAD TO LIE"

"One French agent was caught by the Gestapo, who broke his feet in torturing him. He managed to escape from them and we picked him up and brought him back to England. He could not, of course, make a parachute jump again but he insisted on returning to France. So we took him over. He was a brave man."

How secret it all was may be judged by this - said to me by another of the pilots: "Even when high ranking officers who were not in the know asked us about the work we were doing we had to lie like old Harry. It was court martial for anyone who breathed a word about the job. Not even the mechanics knew about the passenger flights."

In December 2002, again by luck, I made contact with a gentleman named Len Mulholland who lives in British Columbia, Canada. On the night of the 5/6 July 1944 Len, or to give his code name at the time RUMMY, was also being taken by a Hudson, flown by P/O Morris, to be dropped into Holland.

During our recent correspondence Len mentioned an incident that happened to him which is quite amusing now, although I am sure that at the time it was far from funny. Len recounts that one of his duties was to select potential dropping sites and submit them back to London for approval. Should the RAF agree that the sites were suitable then weapons, ammunition and explosives would be dropped there. Len went on to say that some of the sites were used more than once and, in fact, he had one that was used eight times. The eighth time was the last for this site as he recalled; "The last time was when we could see people on the top of the roofs of the houses close by, all yelling: the Allies are coming......the Allies are coming!! This was when we decided not to use that site any more."

I have also been fortunate to make contact with an ex 161 Squadron pilot living on the Isle of Wight, Len Smith DFC. Len too has some memories that I think are worth relating. He tells of a rear gunner, Jasper Matthews, who had a pet dog, a miniature smooth haired terrier that always accompanied him on operations. The WAAFs in the parachute section made the dog its own special parachute. On 16 December 1943 the crew was forced to abandon the aircraft. All landed safely in East Anglia but

Jasper kept his pet secure in his own flying overall as they descended together.

Len also recalls; "Normally operations were limited to the ten day 'moon period', (the period around the full moon). Leave was generous and on my 250 cc Triumph motorcycle I could make it home to Sidcup for the weekend. If I parked near the M.T. Section, in some mysterious way the tank was always full when I came to drive off!".

After a visit to Tempsford airfield in 1976, E. S. Burke wrote a poem that sums up the role played by those stationed there and those who left for an uncertain future from the airfield.

AT TEMPSFORD

1976

In fleeting, darkened hours they met.

By purpose joined together.

With but a word or nod - and yet

their spirits linked forever.

Briefly their lives, the flyers and the "Joes"

Were touched - no drums were rolled.

They have no shrine, but in the

Heart of those of us who care.

To stand at Tempsford, hear the start of

Engines and voices in the air.

TAKING THE WINGS OF THE MORNING

TAKING THE WINGS OF THE MORNING

On the 15 March 1944 Ian was posted, along with F/O Bunney, to 161 Squadron, one of the two Special Duties squadrons (sometimes referred to as the Moonlight Squadrons), based at Tempsford in Bedfordshire. His duties with 161 Squadron were to involve him in two types of operational flying. One was piloting aircraft on "Ascension" flights and the other was the dropping of agents, with their equipment, into occupied Europe. Ascension flights entailed the pilot and crew flying over a designated area, and a wireless operator talking to an agent on the ground. Transmissions normally lasted no longer than half an hour.

Ian joined the Hudson flight and assembled his crew of three. These men were to be his crew for all the operational flights he captained. F/O Kenneth Bunney, who had come to 161 Squadron with him from 1483 TT&G Flight was his Navigator, Sgts Eric Eliot and Dennis Withers,, both already serving on the squadron, became respectively his Rear Gunner and Wireless Operator.

At this point I would like to be able to give a reasonably detailed account of how each crew member came to be on the aircraft that night and some idea of the path they must have followed to arrive at this point in time. However, despite all the research I have done I am afraid that, compared with the information on the Dutch side of the operations, I have very little on the crew of FK790 and their backgrounds; one day, I hope, more will be available. The information that I have gleaned, both from the record books and the relatives of these men is as follows.

TAKING THE WINGS OF THE MORNING

Pilot Officer Kenneth Ralph Bunney

Don Bunney, brother of Kenneth, gave me this information.

"Born on the 22 August 1913 at Crofton Park, South East London. Educated at the local council school and then at Brockly County School.

His sport was rugby. On leaving school he joined the PEARL Assurance Co. And worked in an office at Holborn, London. Here he met the lady who was to become his wife. His spare time interests were mainly cycling and some sea fishing; he had a keen interest in motorcycle sport.

During 1942 Bunney served as a Sgt Navigator with 149 Squadron where he completed a tour of 30 operations. On one occasion, 29 June 1942, he was lucky to survive when the aircraft he was in, a Stirling 1, crashed on take-off. On 2 November 1942, at the end of his tour, he was posted out of the squadron to 1483 Target Towing and Gunnery Flight.

It would have been during this posting that he met Ian. The records show that during his time with 1483 TT&G he was involved in several air/sea rescue missions before, on 15 March 1944, joining, with Ian, 161 (SD) Squadron. On the 5/6 July of that year he was killed in action and is buried at Makkum, Holland.

After a visit to Tempsford during September 2001, Don Bunney and I were talking about how he felt regarding Ken and his duties with the RAF. Don told me that Ken did not tell him what his duties with 161 Squadron involved as he was, obviously, sworn to secrecy but he had guessed that it must be something special. Don went on to say that just prior to the 5 July, Ken had been home for a visit and, when leaving to return to the squadron, at the end of the path Ken turned and waved goodbye; something he had not done previously.

Don says that at that moment, (and he remembers it quite clearly), he had the feeling that this was to be the last time he would see his brother.

TAKING THE WINGS OF THE MORNING

Sergeant Eric Marshall Eliot

While working at Number 2 Technical School at RAF Karachi in the late 1930's, Sgt Eliot took a keen interest in the state of European politics and watched the build up of German forces, ending with the invasion of Poland. During the next few years Sgt Eliot monitored the developments in Europe and, increasingly, felt that he was not contributing enough to the war effort. In 1942 he applied for a transfer back to England and also into aircrew where he thought he could be of more use. His application was accepted and, on his return to England, he was sent on a course to become an Air Gunner.

Little is shown in the records regarding Sgt Eliot's career and I have not been able to find any information prior to his joining 161 Squadron other than he transferred to 161 Sqdn from No. 31 Base.

TAKING THE WINGS OF THE MORNING

Sergeant Dennis James Withers

Sergeant Withers, like Sergeant Eliot, joined 161 (Special Duties) Squadron from 31 Base and, from the records; it appears that he soon "teamed up" with Sergeant Eliot. Before joining Ian's crew he had completed several operations with a variety of different captains.

TAKING THE WINGS OF THE MORNING

Just three weeks before he was killed Dennis was married to Joan. One of the memories Joan recounts is that on D - Day she and Dennis were walking along a road to the vicarage, to collect their Banns, when he remarked to her "You nearly didn't have a husband last night, we landed back with a damaged tail and a broken wing. A tribute to the pilot's skill". Unfortunately, while the record books show a mission for that night, I have been unable to find any combat or damage report.

Joan goes on to relate that after she was informed by Tempsford that the aircraft had not returned from an operation she lived in hope that he was a Prisoner of War. It was to take six months before she heard from the Red Cross informing her that Dennis' body had been found and buried at Makkum.

The mission on 5 April was another Ascension one, this time code named "Roddy"; once again, after a two and a half hour flight the aircraft returned to base with the mission completed.

On 7 April, Ian had his first flight that involved the dropping of supplies to the resistance. It was a Halifax flight, with Ian as second pilot to P/O Smith; the operation code named "John 40", was to drop supplies to a resistance group in France.

Two nights later, Ian was again second pilot on a Halifax, this time captained by F/Sgt McGibbon, on a double operation. The two parts of the operation were code named "Syringa" and "Dick 8"; both were completed successfully. The first leg of the operation (Syringa) involved the dropping of agents, supplies, homing pigeons and leaflets into France. The second part of the operation (Dick 8), also to France, saw 13 containers and four packages dropped successfully. This drop was completed in just six minutes between 02:22 and 02:28. After this operation Ian was to captain his own aircraft for all future operations.

The Ascension flight on 5 May was followed by Ian's first operation, on the night of 6/7 May, as captain of a flight that involved the dropping of agents. There is some dispute about the target area of this operation, code named "Blundells"; the Squadron diary shows the destination as France, yet the pilot's debriefing notes give the area as Holland. When talking to a Dutch researcher some years ago, he told me that there were no drops into Holland that night. However, when one looks at the debriefing form completed by Ian on his return from the mission, Note 4, "(Instructions to Captain of A/C"), the area is clearly shown as Holland. Looking further into the report there is more evidence that this drop did take place in Holland.

The course notes, in the report, show that the aircraft crossed the English coast at Aldeburgh at 00:31 at a height of 2000 feet. Thirty-four minutes later it crossed the Dutch coast and were dropped to a height of 700 feet, six miles from the original target at the request of
the agents, or as Ian records it; "at the request of the Joes".

Further evidence that this drop did in fact go into Holland is demonstrated by the entry in Sgt Withers' log book. Here the date and destination are clearly visible.

Date	Hour	Aircraft Type and No.	Pilot	Duty	Remarks (including results of bombing, gunnery, exercises, etc.)	Flying Times Day	Night
					Time carried forward:—	122.55	98.55
1.5.44	23.15	Hudson 'N'	F/Lt. Menzies	W.op	Exercise (Scrubbed)		
3.5.44	23.30	Hudson 'P'	F/Lt Menzies	W.op	Exercise		1.40
5.5.44	17.00	Hudson 'L'	F/Lt Menzies	W.op	Operations as detailed	2.35	
6.5.44	23.06	Hudson 'N'	F/Lt. Menzies	W.op	Operations (Holland) D.C.O. (3)		2.25
8.5.44	22.20	Hudson 'N'	F/Lt. Menzies	W.op	Operations France D.C.O. (4)		6.25
10.5.44	24.00	Hudson 'N'	F/Lt Menzies	W.op	Dropping Exercise		1.00
13.5.44	11.30	Hudson 'M'	F/Lt. Menzies	W.op	To Prestwick and Return	4.25	
15.5.44	14.30	Hudson 'N'	F/Lt Menzies	W.op	Fighter Affiliation	.35	
15.5.44	15.20	Hudson 'R'	S/Ldr Wilkinson	W.op	Fighter Affiliation	.50	
22.5.44	16.30	Hudson 'Q'	F/Lt Menzies	W.op	To Middle Wallop & Return	1.30	
23.5.44	10.50	Hudson 'O'	Cdr Cerby	W.op	To Sherburn in Elmet & Return	2.25	
					Total Time:—	135.35	111.45

It would certainly appear that the misunderstanding about this drop is within the Dutch records as a second Hudson from 161 Squadron also went to Holland that night, according to the pilot's notes. F/Sgt Ron Morris, flying Hudson M, reported that he made his dummy run from Breda to his target, where he dropped the agents for the operation code named "St. Valentine". Here is a clue within the notes as to the confusion surrounding these missions to Holland. F/Sgt Morris' notes explain that he had to bring back the 15 pigeons he was due to drop as they had, in his words, "French markings". In January 2002 I spoke with Ron who remembers this flight very clearly. Without any prompting he told me about the pigeons and the reason for them being brought back to England.

On 8 May, Ian and his crew were dispatched on a double mission, "Lalaie" and "Minister 3", both to France. The first part of the operation, "Lalaie", was completed when at 01:37 the one agent on board was dropped, from 800 feet, on the target that had been identified by reception lights, although they were slightly to the East of the pinpoint. The second half of the mission, "Minister 3", (one agent and three packages) was not completed as the reception was incorrect. Ian's remarks, in the debriefing notes, say that after making a dummy run a fire was seen at the estimated site of the target. Slightly to the North West of the fire was a semicircle of lights incorporating what looked rather like a reception. As he made his run in the lights were extinguished.

Under item 10 of this report, "Enemy Opposition.", Ian has made an entry that makes one wonder if he had a lucky escape. It says that while in the Chateaudun area at 03:00 and at 5,000 feet, two JU88's or Messerschmidt ME210's were positioned astern at a distance of 200 - 300 yards and one ME109 "shot under going in opposite direction". There is no note of what, if any, action was taken. As the weather conditions were hazy it is possible that the Germans mistook the Hudson for one of their own aircraft.

The next operation, still in May, for the crew was an unsuccessful Ascension mission, code named "Nylon". Radio contact had been established but because of a faulty fuel pump the operation had to be abandoned. The next "moon period" was in early June and the dropping of agents began again. On the eve of D-Day, 5/6 June, Ian and his crew were operational again, this time with a mission named "Westminster".

After taking off from Tempsford the aircraft crossed the English coast at 00:17 and then, 30 minutes later, the Dutch coast at Tholen at a height of just 50 feet. From here the course took them across country, passing over Rossum, still at only 50 feet, where one searchlight was observed. Shortly after this they passed over the railway bridge at Zalt-Bommel, again at an altitude of only 50 feet, where they encountered one searchlight and light flak from six guns.

The Dutch researcher Aad Neeven supplied me with information regarding the Dutch side of the operation which was as follows.

The two Dutch agents involved in this drop were Frans Dijckmeester and K. Chr. Mooiweer. There was a problem with the slide, used for the despatch of agents; this caused the agents to be slightly late exiting the aircraft. Dijckmeester was the first to jump but, because of the delay, landed some five kilometres from the target area. This was not the only problem for him. The line securing his leg bag did not free itself properly and therefore his leg bag did not fall, to its proper position, some distance below him, but stayed between his feet. On landing the bag split open and the contents were strewn around the field. As a result of the delay in exiting the aircraft Mooiweer landed some 15 kilometres from his target area and he too had problems; landing in the middle of a ditch near the village of Waardeburg. Fortunately the radios he was carrying were not damaged. Eventually, with some assistance both agents ended up at the village of Buurmalsen. Although they were soon parted both agents went on to provide a valuable service to the resistance.

The night of 7/8 June came and Ian and his crew were operational, flying Hudson MA-R, the aircraft in which they were to make their final flight, on a mission code named "Restinga 1", to France. This time they crossed the English coast, at Lyme Regis, at 01:13, and then flew on into France. After making a dummy run from Ploermel, two packages and 15 pigeons were dropped at 02:52. Ian reports that, after the drop was made, the doors jammed and the aircraft made a wide circuit over the target area. Ian states that there was "No doubt of position, clearly identified by ground detail, although without good moon some difficulty may be found getting in exact position".

After this trip the crew did not fly operationally until 28 June when it was another Ascension flight. This time it was code named "Westminster" and was unsuccessful as no contact was made.

The night of 29 June had an operation, "Frederick 2", involving the use of two aircraft from the Hudson flight. Ian's Hudson, FK790 again, was the second of the two aircraft to take-off. The target area for the night was France with Ian and his crew making a drop of eight packages. This time it was a low level drop, from just 200 feet. The aircraft homed in on the drop zone using GEE and picked up the lights of the reception, three bonfires in a row, and a clear identification signal was flashed. The weather was bad at the time and the crew had trouble getting the aircraft low enough to get a clear view of the reception. After an initial dummy run the drop was made from only 200 feet, however one package got stuck making a third run necessary to complete the operation.

The first operational flight of July was a double Ascension mission, "Student" and "Braid", which was unsuccessful. A 20 minute delay arriving in the patrol area was caused by bad weather. As a result, despite remaining in the area and trying for one hour, no contact was made.

The next operation was to be a drop of agents into Holland. On the 5/6 July, Ian and his crew left Tempsford, with four agents, on what was to be their final flight.

TAKING THE WINGS OF THE MORNING

TAKING THE WINGS OF THE MORNING

5/6 JULY 1944

Jan Bockma

Aged 22 years, the son of a prominent resistance leader did much to aid the efforts of the resistance but he felt that he could do more. With this thought in mind he decided to come to England, but his father disagreed with Jan, saying that he would be of more use in Holland. However, Jan was determined to have his way and on 16 May 1942 he left to come to England. Having first travelled to Spain he came in contact with the

Foreign Legion, which he joined. Sometime later he deserted and managed to get to the UK on board a Norwegian boat, arriving in England a year after he had left Holland, on 16 May 1943. After a time in the Navy (Dutch?), he joined the BBO and trained as a Wireless Operator; eventually he was given a mission and was to be returned to Holland on the first "moon period" of July 1944. The first available date was 5 July.

The name of his operation, and which he would be known by at his station of departure (Tempsford), was "Halma". This was not to be used in the field. While on operations in the field, working as wireless operator to Verhoef (Racquets) his name was "Hubertus".

The intention of Jan's mission was to make contact with the RVV (Raad Van Verzet - part of the Dutch underground movement). He was to inform them that his mission was to act as W/T operator for their sabotage organisation for all their communications with the appropriate authorities back in England. He was not to be involved in any of their other activities. Jan was also instructed that he was to supply his contacts with, and teach them how to use, the special One-Time code pads; at all times he was to observe security instructions given to him by the RVV, and never to make contacts other than those arranged by the RVV Jan was also instructed to insist that the RVV arrange for a "safe house" for him and houses from where he could transmit.

A small paragraph in Jan's instructions advises that he was to carry "an extra W/T plan and a small code for the use of a new operator if the RVV or you can find a man who is considered 100% safe. You may train him and advise us when he is ready to operate".

The method of Jan's operation was given in his briefing notes showing that he was to be dropped with Pleun Verhoef and two others. Instructions stated that he should, upon landing, immediately bury or destroy his parachute equipment and then bury his W/T equipment separately but in such a way that a third party would be able to find it if, when the time came to collect it, it was considered unsafe for him to go in person.

Along with his radio equipment Jan was also issued with a sum of money, Hfl150 of it in small change and a further Hfl4,500 to be carried in his briefcase. Further money in the form of Belgian and French Francs was concealed in a money belt. Also he carried a spare One-Time pad which he should give to the RVV, but not until they had asked for it. One further item, carried by Jan, was a silenced .32 hand gun with 50 rounds of ammunition which was to be given to Pleun Verhoef.

When it came to communications, Jan was given many instructions and details on topics covering Codes, Prefixes, Broadcasts, Safety Checks, Code Poems and Safe Houses.

Item six on his mission notes confirms his rank as Second Lieutenant and that his salary would be paid to the Dutch Government. The details of his mission, having been read, were signed as "Understood" by Jan using another of his code names (J Borel) and dated "London 27 June 1944".

TAKING THE WINGS OF THE MORNING

Pleun Verhoef

After the surrender of the Dutch Army, of which he was a member, the 24 year old Pleun managed to escape to England by way of Belgium and France. For a time he was placed in a tented camp at Porthcawl before being moved to Congleton and then on to Wrottesley Park (near Wolverhampton). At Wrottesley Park, on 27 August 1941, Queen Wilhelmina issued the colours of the Royal Dutch Brigade Princess Irene.

Pleun joined one of the units within the brigade, the parachute unit. He passed through his training, getting good marks for his five training jumps. He then progressed, getting his Corporal's stripes on the way, to training with explosives in October 1941. On 2 April 1942 he left the brigade to go to the SOE for training but ended up working for the Dutch BBO organisation.

Prior to his despatch to Holland Pleun, like the three other agents, was given specific and detailed instructions. The operational name, and the name he would be known by at Tempsford, was "Racquets" and his code name in the field was to be Eitjes. The background information that Pleun was given included the facts that the RVV, the organisation to which he was going, had had some of its cells penetrated from time to time. He was also informed that an earlier mission, sent to the field on 1 April 1944 had been arrested between 17 May and 20 May that year. That earlier mission had, contrary to instructions, contacted several other organisations and was known to the Gestapo. Therefore the RVV had reported the arrests and requested that new men be sent.

The purpose of Verhoef's mission was to make contact with the RVV at a given address from where he would be put in contact with the heads of the local groups. Pleun's instructions were that, once in contact with the

RVV leaders, he should inform them that his mission was to act as their saboteur instructor and/or Reception Committee leader. The exact role would depend on the immediate requirement.

As with Bockma, Verhoef was given specific instructions regarding security. He was never to make contact with other organisations unless the meeting had been arranged by the local RVV. Also, under no circumstances should he reveal the fact that he had come from England to anyone and at all times he should obey instructions given to him by the RVV. This message was reinforced by a note saying that the men who went to Holland on 1 April had not followed these instructions and had been arrested.

The instructions for his mission continued saying that he was to "assist the RVV and advise them on all matters in which you have received your instruction in this country". He was to insist that he was found safe houses from which to operate and, when arranging their sabotage organisation it was to be in such a way as to neither clash with nor compromise their other activities. Furthermore he was not to overburden his W/T Operator (Jan Bockma) with messages, nor should he get involved with matters of intelligence; his mission was not connected with intelligence gathering and if London wanted any information they would ask for it.

Detailed instructions were given regarding Reception Committees. These covered such matters as the suitability and recruitment of personnel for the committee, always bearing in mind the need for security; the selection of grounds for the drops and the number of containers that could safely be handled by that committee. Plus, of course, the maps and co-ordinates that should be used for any drop and the identification lighting that should be used.

Like Bockma, Verhoef was given instructions on the disposal of his parachute equipment and advised of the money he would be carrying. His cover story, clothing, equipment for the field, documents and routes of return to the UK were also given to him.

Pleun, too, was issued with a sum of money, some for his personal use (Hfl1,500) and also 2,500 French Francs plus 2,500 Belgian Francs for emergency use. In addition both he and Kwint (BAREND) were to take Hfl25,000 each, concealed in money belts, making a total of Hfl50,000 which was for the RVV. This money was not to be handed over until they were asked by a representative of the organisation who would prove their identity by asking for Hfl50,001, a simple check to ensure the money went to the correct recipient.

Pleun was given further special instructions regarding communications. In the field he was to employ the various methods he had been taught; post boxes, cut-outs etc. He was advised that his messages would not be sent by him directly to his wireless operator but had to be passed through the RVV for forwarding to the operator. Instructions stated that all encoding and decoding of his messages was to be done by him and that the part of the One-Time pad which had been used for messages must be destroyed. Under no circumstances should records of messages exchanged be kept.

The heading of "Communications" also covered topics such as: Innocent Letters - their address and signature, BBC Messages - these would be broadcast on stated days - safe houses and identity checks - if London had reason to suppose he was in German hands they would ask an "innocent" question. If they did not receive the correct answer it would confirm that he had been captured. Pigeons: he was to take a carrier pigeon with him which could be released on landing and thus advise of his safe arrival. Further pigeons would be supplied and then used to send back long and coded messages, film, negatives, printed matter and so forth.

Verhoef was also given some further instructions about two Eureka radio sets (Nos 562 and 563) that were to be dropped to the RVV, and which would form part of his mission. He was told to place these two sets as near as possible to two locations of which he would be advised. As it would be almost impossible, due to his other activities, to operate the sets throughout the moon periods, he was to recruit and train two men solely in the use of these sets. This was to be done in consultation with the RVV. Furthermore he would be supplied with a list of code signals for each set and the type of BBC message that would be broadcast.

The type of BBC message for each set would be explained later in a wireless message. The purpose of the two Eureka sets was to assist the RAF in their efforts both in dropping agents into Holland and bombing operations over Germany.

His notes concluded by saying that on leaving the country he would be accorded the rank of second Lieutenant and his salary credited to the Dutch Government. These instructions were dated 26 June 1944.

Peter Kwint

Peter Kwint was studying at the University of Amsterdam when he was required to sign a declaration of loyalty to the Germans. He refused to do this and went into hiding in Dreibergen and joined the underground movement. After a time he decided he would be better off coming to England and so he departed Amsterdam on 8 November 1943. He travelled to Paris on false papers and, on arrival, managed to obtain food and shelter. From Paris he went to the German border. On 19 December 1943, when he was on Spanish soil, he was arrested by the local police and ended up in the prison at Figueras. After a few days he was visited by a Dutch official who informed him that they were working on his release. The conditions in the prison were very bad; it was crowded, dirty, with no medical assistance and poor food. On 29 December 1943 Kwint was handcuffed with many others and, in pairs, they were put aboard a train bound for Barcelona. After an exhausting trip they were locked up in a cellar; the next day the same procedure, from Barcelona to Reus, and again into prison. It was New Year's Eve. From here they were transferred to a cell in Saragossa where they were locked up again. On 3 January 1944 he was posted to the Camp Miranda de Ebro. After what they had been through in the prisons this was not too bad. The release came quicker than they had expected. On 19 January Kwint went by train to Madrid, and after he reported to the Dutch consulate he went to town to buy clothing and shoes. With a large group of about 100 people Kwint was transported through Spain to Portugal and put on board the ship "Ondura". On 16 March 1944 the ship dropped anchor in Liverpool; a difficult journey had been completed.

After the usual interrogation at the Patriotic School, which was not difficult for Kwint due to his resistance background, they asked him to join the Secret Service (SOE) and to be dropped into Holland. He joined the BBO, got the code name Pieter Krant and, following good marks with the agent training, he was promoted on 3 July 1944 to 2nd Lieutenant in the Special Services. Kwint's mission was very similar to that of Pleun Verhoef; he was given the same stern warning at the beginning of his briefing notes, regarding the fact that an earlier mission had failed because of the lack of proper security precautions. Again, like the others, he too had more than one name, one for use at Tempsford, which was FIVES, and another for use in the field which was BAREND.

Kwint, like Verhoef, was going into Holland as a saboteur instructor and/or Reception Committee organiser. Kwint's instructions only differed from those of Verhoef's in two ways; one was that when he collected his gun and ammunition, in Kwint's case, from Walter, he was also to receive a white envelope marked with a circle. This envelope was to be kept carefully and safely until instructions were received for its disposal. No further mention of this envelope has been found and so the contents still remain a mystery.

The second difference between Kwint's instructions and Verhoef's was that Kwint did not have the added responsibility that went with the two Eureka sets.

Once again the need for security was heavily emphasised by stressing that only those people of whom he had or could obtain full knowledge of should form a Reception Committee.

He was reminded that the maps that were to be used to supply the co-ordinates for the landing areas were to be taken from the map of the Netherlands that had a scale of 1:50,000. Should these maps be unavailable he was to use another type, which he had been trained to use, ensuring that he gave the distance and bearing of two villages. Also, when transmitting the co-ordinates for drops or landings he must always include the series number of maps that he was using. Simple and common-sense tasks perhaps, but ones which incorrectly performed could lead to disaster.

Johannes Walter

Aged 21, he was born at Djambang, Java. Walter had served in the Navy until 1 January 1942 and on 3 May he arrived in England. He left the Navy and went on a wireless operators' course, with the RAF, at Blackpool. Sometime around June 1943 he was approached by the SOE who asked him if he would work for them as a wireless operator. This he accepted and was released from the Navy to perform this new role. After a short period of training, with the BBO, he qualified as a W/T Operator for them. While he was in England he married an English girl named Margaret who, when Johannes left for Holland, was expecting their child.

As with the other agents, Walter was given several different names, for use in different areas of his activities. The name of his operation and the name for use at the station of departure, Tempsford, was Bowls. During his time in the field his code-name was to be Albertus.

His mission instructions were to act as W/T Operator to Verhoef and the rest of his instructions were almost a duplicate of those given to Bockma but with two exceptions. Firstly his personal baggage consisted of one brown paper parcel and secondly he was to carry the mysterious "white envelope marked with a circle".

General Instructions

An annexe to the orders for the four agents contained instructions for the first stage of their missions; to make their way to the contact address.

They were informed that they were to be dropped at a point on the APPELSCHE HEIDE on sheet 32 AMERSFOORT an area to the NE of Utrecht. After burying their kit and equipment they were to make their way to the contact address, approximately one kilometre from where they had been dropped. The address given in this annexe to orders is:

> Boerderij van der Zalm,
> Landbouw School
> APPELSCHE HEIDE.

When they made contact here they should use the password "Ik kom voor de Volkestelling 1945", which translated into English means "I've come for the 1945 Census".

To assist these agents in their work in the field they would have been given instruction in various types of sabotage which would have included not only physical sabotage but also ways of strengthening morale amongst the local population. At the same time efforts would have been made to undermine the morale of the occupying forces.

A few examples of physical sabotage are given below; they have been taken from a paper entitled, "AIRCRAFT SABOTAGE: ACTION AND RESULTS".

TAKING THE WINGS OF THE MORNING

Take the split pins from the main landing wheel retaining nuts. Loosen the nuts to such a degree as to make sure they will come undone as the aircraft moves.

Result: This will enable the landing wheel to come off as the aircraft taxis or takes off.

Put sugar in the petrol tank.

Result: the engines will stop after about two hours flying.
Or, perhaps more seriously: Loosen the engine bearer bolts to such an extent that they are just holding on. Result: This will cause the engine to vibrate violently and may even cause it to fall off.

Some examples of the more subtle, yet no less important, methods of sabotage, those affecting the morale of both sides, follow.

Organising regular listening service to Allied radio broadcasts to ensure up to date news was available to counter rumours spread by the Germans.

To obstruct enemy and quisling activities by exerting pressure on known traitors to ensure they disclose information.

Spread the slogan that he who does not actively prove himself on the side of the Allies will afterwards be assumed to have been against them.

To undermine enemy troop morale. Use any means to depress and unnerve enemy troops such as:
(a) Circulate news of military events with emphasis on details of German losses.
(b) Irritation and exasperation of local German troops with a view to producing indiscipline.

So, now safely in Britain, trained to the high standards that were required, primed with the information necessary to undertake the hazardous work ahead of them, the agents were ready to proceed to the next stage. This stage was to get them all together in a holding area, a safe house, near their point of departure, Tempsford in Bedfordshire. In the case of these four agents the safe house was, most likely, Hassell's Hall.

5/6 July 1944

The time the agents had at the house would have allowed them to go over their instructions and cover stories, and familiarise themselves with the identities they would adopt once in the field.

The first indication of the arrival of their departure date was often the provision of two eggs with their evening meal. During a period of severe rationing for the rest of the country such luxuries bore a special significance.

As their departure time drew closer they were taken by car, some lucky ones in the luxury of a blacked-out Rolls Royce, to the airfield at Gibraltar Farm. Once there they went to the barn where their clothing was checked to ensure that it was appropriate for the country that was their destination and that there were no labels or laundry marks that would betray them. The four of them then took possession of the documents made out to support their new identities and the cash that they would need for their immediate use. Field equipment was checked and issued; Walter and Bockma received their radios and pistols plus the substantial amount of money destined for the resistance; Kwint and Verhoef checked on the explosives and detonators they would be taking. When all this had been done, with meticulous care, and their parachutes issued they were ready to start the next stage of their journey.

At some point, during the afternoon of 5 July, Flt. Lt. Menzies would have found, from information posted in the dispersal hut, that he and his crew were to be flying that night. The crew then had a few hours to while away before the briefings that had to take place. A few hours in which to catch some sleep, write a letter home or, perhaps, just spend some time in quiet reflection before once again venturing forth by the light of the moon.

At the briefing the crew were informed that they would be carrying four agents, some packages and homing pigeons which were to be released by the agents once they had landed safely. To go with this information they received the dropping zone co-ordinates, recognition signals and code-words to be used during the mission. Now it was time to prepare the aircraft and await the arrival of their passengers.

For the agents: their journey to the waiting aircraft started when a WAAF driver brought a car to the barn to collect them; she would have been under no illusion regarding the importance of the security that was required. One of these drivers recalled the instructions she had been given regarding the conveyance of the agents to waiting aircraft. She said that the car was driven up to the barn where she had to wait, eyes facing front, while the passengers were ushered into the rear of the vehicle. Under no circumstances was she to talk to the passengers or turn around to look at them and the use of the rear view mirror was forbidden. As she obeyed these instructions to the letter, to this day she does not know who she ferried out to the waiting aircraft, not even if they were male or female.

Once at the aircraft the car had to be reversed up to the door of the aircraft using only wing mirrors, no use of the rear view mirror or turning around to see out of the back window. A tricky manoeuvre made more difficult by the palpable tension within the vehicle. The rear doors of the car were opened by a waiting crew member and the agents exited the vehicle leaving the driver to return to her station.

The crew member who took charge of the agents was most likely to have been Dennis Withers. As he was the wireless operator he would be the crew member who was least likely to be engaged in other duties when they were approaching the drop zone and he would therefore double as the Despatcher, the only crew member to meet the agents.

There is some confusion as to the time of departure of the aircraft, with records showing three different times. The typed form prepared for the pilot's debriefing after the mission shows a take-off time of 23:47. The copy of 161 Squadron Battle Orders for that night (again a typed entry) shows take-off 23:50. The handwritten entry in the Operational Record book shows a take off at 01:50 (morning of the 6 July) some two hours later. There is no mention of a reason for a delay if indeed there was one. However, if this entry is correct the delay *may* be connected with the events that happened a little later.

TAKING THE WINGS OF THE MORNING

With permission to take off granted by the control tower, the Hudson accelerated down the runway and took off, heading east, into a bright moonlit night. On board the aircraft, illuminated only by the lights of the instrument panels, the crew went about their routine tasks. This was their sixth operation involving the dropping of agents into enemy occupied territory. For Bockma, Kwint, Verhoef and Walter this was a time of mixed emotions, the culmination of all their training and the reason they had made their way, by their different routes, to Britain. They were, at last, on their way back to their mother country, Holland.

Crossing the coast at Aldeburgh, F/O Bunney informed the pilot of the course to take them on the first leg of their journey, over the North Sea, flying at extremely low level, towards the Friesian islands. Also flying a Hudson that night, on another mission to Holland, was Flt Sgt Ron Morris. Ron has explained to me that, to avoid the risk of being picked up on enemy radar, he never flew higher than ten feet on this part of the journey!

Approaching the Friesian islands of Texel, Vlieland, Terschelling and Ameland, Bunney plotted the next part of their journey, taking them between two of the islands, across the Wadden Sea, up and over the causeway (Afsluitdijk) and down the centre of the IJselmeer to Nijkerk, the destination that was never reached.

At the German airfield in Leeuwarden a night fighter was being held in readiness; seated in a Messerschmidt Bf 110G-4, was Feldwebel Heinrich Lahmann (pilot) and his crew, awaiting further instructions. In the very early hours of the morning the call came through for them to get airborne to intercept an incoming aircraft.

Once in the air contact was made with their ground radar station and they were directed to reference EM8 on the German map, an area near Terschelling. Directions for course and height were received.

In a telephone interview in April 2001, the gunner of the Messerschmitt described the events that followed to Huub van Sabben, a Dutch researcher. He reported that contact was made with the British aircraft, which at the time they thought to be a Lancaster (perhaps because of the twin tail fins). Lahmann reported PAUKE, PAUKE, PAUKE (I'm attacking). Here the gunner adds that the British aircraft "was still not flying at a great height". This conflicts with Ron Morris' comments regarding the height they flew at; there should not have been enough room for the fighter to get underneath to use his upward firing cannons.

TAKING THE WINGS OF THE MORNING

So, a second odd occurrence; what had caused the Hudson to climb, thus allowing this manoeuvre? However it appears that there was enough clear air for the Messerschmitt to get below the Hudson and open fire. The German gunner informed Huub that the British aircraft "was approaching our aircraft fast". He says they decided to fly under the Hudson and as they did so they opened fire with the upward firing cannons. To do this successfully, the German must have turned and opened fire while flying in the same direction as FK790 as the upwards firing cannons faced forward. The gunner says that after opening fire Lahmann "banked away to port to avoid debris from the Hudson which, by now, was on fire. This remark suggests to me that the Messerschmitt was indeed following the Hudson at this time. However, there is another question about this attack; the 20 mm cannons on the night fighter were angled upwards at 70° and yet the evident shell damage to the Hudson propeller (recovered in 1997 and now erected as a monument in Exmorra) shows that the shell passed through, from back to front, almost horizontally.

At this stage of the interview it appears that the gunner has made a mistake regarding the identity of the aircraft they shot down that night. However, he went on to ask Huub if he knew about the secret agents on board; no mention of agents had been made up until now. The gunner explained that after landing back at Leeuwarden and being debriefed he, and the rest of the crew, were instructed to report to the Gruppenkommandeur. He tells that almost all the senior staff of the base was present at this meeting. The first question "What do you think you shot down last night?" was fired at them. Immediately the crew were worried that they had shot down one of their own aircraft, something another crew had done recently. Then it was explained to them that this aircraft had been expected! Instructions had been issued, but not received by Lahmann and his crew, that the Hudson was not to be attacked until after the four agents had jumped. The agents would then have been arrested at the dropping zone. The gunner went on to say that later he had heard that there were four crew plus four agents on board the aircraft so perhaps it was because of this total of eight that he still thought of a Lancaster, although a Lancaster normally carried a crew of seven. Having been hit by cannon fire, and now on fire, the aircraft was seen to crash into the IJselmeer, some four hundred metres from the Afsluitdijk. The wreckage went straight to the bottom and the waters closed over it. There were no survivors.

AFTER THE CRASH

&

THE "SASKIA SPIEL"

(A disaster avoided)

TAKING THE WINGS OF THE MORNING

Back in England a telegram was delivered to No. 5 Holmwood Gardens, Wallington. The contents of that, most dreaded, telegram stated clearly and concisely; "Regret to inform you that your son Flight Lieutenant J. W. Menzies 108868 is reported missing as the result of air operations on the night of 5th July 1944. Letter follows. Any further information received will be communicated to you immediately pending receipt of written confirmation from the air ministry. No information should be given to the press. O/C no. 161 Squadron." This was closely followed by a letter from the Squadron Padre E P Richardson, who expressed sympathy and the hope that Ian may have been made a prisoner of war. He went on to say "I have known your son ever since he has been on this station and, with all those who knew him, have grown to admire the splendid qualities of his character." All in all, a letter that expressed both sympathy and empathy, trying very hard to give support, albeit from a distance.

Over the course of the next three weeks the waters of the IJselmeer gave up six of the eight bodies. The first body to be recovered was that of Sgt Eliot air gunner), washed ashore, near Gaadst, to the south of Makkum, on 12 July 1944. Three days later the body of the wireless operator, Sgt Withers, was found near Makkum. The body of the third crew member, F/O Bunney, was recovered nearly three weeks after the crash at

TAKING THE WINGS OF THE MORNING

Kornwerderzand. The body of Flt Lt Menzies was not to be found for a further 53 years.

The first body of an agent to be recovered was that of Johannes Walter. On 14 July, he was found floating by a local fisherman, Eelke van de Laan. The body was brought ashore at Makkum and, on the following day, was examined by a German doctor. During the course of the day, 15 July, another fisherman found the body of Peter Kwint. As with the body of Walter, Kwint's body was brought to the mortuary at Makkum to await examination by the German doctor.

Both of these bodies were clad in flying clothes with suits on underneath. Prior to the German doctor's examination a senior police officer, Abele Scheepvaart, a man who was heavily involved with the local resistance group, had checked the bodies and had realised that these men had not been just aircrew, but Dutch agents. However, the German doctor's opinion was different. As the bodies had flying overalls on, with no insignia of rank, he assumed that they had been aircrew undergoing training. In the case of Walter the cause of death was put down to a bullet wound to the head and for Kwint, because there were no visible injuries, death by drowning was recorded. Both were buried, following the post mortem, in Makkum cemetery. Jan Bockma was the next of the agents to be recovered; he was found floating by another fisherman, Jan Bootsma on 24 July. When Bootsma found the body it was still attached to the aircraft by a wire, most likely the static line of his parachute and a brown case was still tied to his body by a scarf. Once again Scheepvaart received the body at Makkum and notified the German authorities. A different doctor arrived to conduct the post mortem this time, a member of the German security service.

When he found the suit beneath the flying clothes he immediately became suspicious and had the clothing removed for further examination. Jan Bockma, although not yet identified, was buried in Makkum cemetery the following morning.

When Bockma's clothing was removed the German doctor found the money belt he was carrying and the papers he had with him. From the evidence now in their possession, the suit under the flying clothes, the money belt and papers the Germans realised that they had the body of an agent. The Germans then returned to Makkum to re-examine the bodies of the other two, Kwint and Walter. When the bodies were exhumed and the flying clothes and suits removed money belts were found on both of them. Kwint's belt contained the 25,000 guilders he had been given in England.

TAKING THE WINGS OF THE MORNING

A report states that on Walter's body was a smaller belt that contained both the money he had been supplied with in England and a small, tightly soldered, tin. The contents of this tin, when opened, caused a certain amount of excitement amongst the Germans but what were the contents? The answer possibly lies in the events that took place later in the month. The body of the fourth agent, Verhoef, was recovered when, in November 1945, the Germans succeeded in raising a part of the aircraft.

Suspect transmission

On 28 July SOE in London received a message which had been transmitted in the code that was Bowls'. The message was transmitted by a person who claimed that he was an anti-Nazi but had been forced into assisting the Gestapo with their counter intelligence work. The message received by London on 28 July was as follows:

"HAVE BEEN FOR OVER 15 YEARS IN ARGENTINA AND U.S.A. WAS PRESSED INTO SERVICE WITH THE GESTAPO AT WAR BEGIN WHILE VISITING IN GERMANY AND AMONG OTHERS GOT TO BE ENTRUSTED WITH TRANSLATING YOUR AGENTS MATERIALS REGISTERING AND FILING PICKED UP AGENTS SENDING SETS. HAVE SINCE LEARNED SIGS IN

(GABITHAVILDWU) BEEN LOOKING FOR A CONTACT CHANCE AS I GOT UTMOSTLY DISGUSTED WITH THIS DAMNED HITLERISM AND LIFE AMONGST THESE IDIOTS HAVE JUST BEEN TRANSLATING MATERIAL FROM THREE OF YOUR AGENTS WHO WERE FOUND DROWNED AT MAKKUM AM CONSIDERED STUPID ENOUGH TO BE HARMLESS SHALL SHOW THEM WANT TO HELP AND WORK WITH YOU GIVE ME A CHANCE PLEASE I SHALL PROVE MY SINCERITY. WHAT MUST YOU KNOW ABOUT ME TO PROVE MYSELF SHALL COME BACK THIRTY FIRST AT PRESCRIBED TIME AND AWAIT YOUR ANSWER THEN."

None of the agents' security checks had been used in this message. How did the sender of the message know that the next transmission date was the thirty-first unless he/she somehow had got hold of the agents' schedules and the crystal?

After the painful experience inflicted by the "England Spiel", (when the Germans had been sending messages that were supposed to be coming from agents in the field to London and London, missing or ignoring the fact that certain safety checks were not as they should be, had acted on these requests, with disastrous consequences), SOE in London were now suspicious of the message received.

It is highly unlikely that something as important as the radio crystal would have been left where this person, so willing to help, could have had access to it. Yet the message received in London had been sent using Bowls' (Walters) crystal; was it the Germans trying the same trick again? Was the reason for the Germans delight on finding the contents of the tin carried by Walter the fact that it contained the crystal and radio codes?

London decided to continue with the exchange of messages, while bearing in mind what had happened before, as there was, of course, the chance that the sender was genuine. They replied to his question of what he had to do to prove his "sincerity" by asking for his full name, date of birth and the dates of his stays in Argentina and the USA. Further information required, by London, was the details of the three agents drowned at Makkum and the number of the set he was using for transmission. Furthermore they asked for details of agents, sent from England, who had been arrested in the last six months.

The reply came back saying his name was Johann Blanke plus, as requested, his date of birth and his times in Buenos Aries and New York.

He gave the names of the three agents at Makkum as Pieter Nijhof (Kwint), Johannes Kamp (Walter) and Jan Boersma (Bockma) and said that no radio set had been found, only the crystal. Blanke then asked if he could have more convenient transmission times, say between 13:00 and 15:00 local time. He sent in a report with the names of six agents who had been arrested between the beginning of February and the middle of July 1944 and also asked London for a new radio set, code, transmission plan and code poem, explaining that to keep going as he was would inevitably lead to discovery and arrest.

SOE, in London, thanked him for the names of the arrested agents but added that there was still more to do before he had their confidence; they now wanted to know the codes of the radio sets, in Gestapo hands, that were being used to transmit back to London. They understood his position and, for the meantime, he should keep his transmissions to a minimum. When they were satisfied with him an arrangement would be made to get new equipment to him. Blanke replied to London saying that his list was incomplete as he was not the only translator engaged in this type of work and therefore he could only answer questions about the cases with which he was involved.

Radio transmissions between London and Blanke continued for some months until SOE sent a message terminating the contact. This breaking of contact was to be proved the right thing to have done when, after the war, it was found that the German SD was behind the transmissions. The officer handling the operation was one SS - Scharfurher Otto Houbrouk who had given it the codename "Saskiaspiel". The character Johannes Blanke did actually exist; he worked with the SD in The Hague.

Obviously, London had learned from their earlier experience with the "Englandspiel" and had, by their caution, avoided a repeat of that disaster. There are still some questions that need answers but will most probably remain unanswered. How did the Germans know the aircraft was coming? Was it by a radio signal intercept or by something more sinister? The German air gunner says he fired his cannons at the Hudson; this would normally have been done from position *beneath* the target aircraft. The damage to the propeller shows the *horizontal* path of a 20 mm cannon shell, from the back to the front of the front of the blade. What had caused Ian to take the Hudson to a height that would make it visible to the enemy radar? Agent Walter died from a gun shot wound to the head, did that shot come from the Messerschmitt?

TAKING THE WINGS OF THE MORNING

Even after all these years of research, with so much being discovered, it seems that the end will stay somewhat shrouded in mystery. However one thing is certain that is on the night of 5/6 July 1944 four highly trained aircrew and four brave and determined young Dutchmen lost their lives.

1998

THE SECOND ENDING

Around April 1998 I heard from Klaas. He informed me that the propeller which had been recovered from the wreckage had been cleaned and was to be mounted on a plinth, as a permanent memorial, in the village of Exmorra. This was the village in the area where it was thought, (incorrectly), that the agents were to have been dropped. Klaas told me that there was to be an official unveiling of the propeller; both Derek and I were invited to attend the ceremony.

Arrangements were quickly put in place and once more I returned to Holland, meeting Derek, Daphne his wife, and his sister and brother-in-law Fay and Peter, at a hotel in Makkum. It seemed that no sooner had we reached Makkum than we were off to Exmorra. Here Derek and I were in for a surprise. We were there not just to attend the ceremony but to play a large part in the proceedings. Klaas sprang the surprise on us by telling us that there was to be a march, from a muster point in the village, to the square where the propeller had been mounted and that Derek and I were to lead the parade. Then, at the appropriate time, we would perform the unveiling of the monument. The propeller had had part of a resistance parachute attached to the tip of one of the blades and then two pegs fixed the rest of the 'chute to the ground. The idea was that at the right time Derek and I would release the parachute from the top of the blade thus unveiling the monument. All went well, but only just. The top of the propeller blade was a long way off the ground and neither Derek nor I are tall, and even with the help of a pole, this was not the easiest task to perform!

A short service followed and a small reception in the local school. It was here that I met the relatives of two more of the agents, Kwint and Verhoef. So I now had the relatives of all those who had been on board Hudson FK790, with the exception of Johannes Walter.

I think that it was also about this time that I heard from Insworth, (for years now I have kicked myself for not keeping a diary of events and record of conversations). I was informed that, at last, a positive identification had been made and that the remains were indeed those of Ian. Although the RAF dental records had been destroyed, the records of the South Staffordshire Regiment, the Army regiment Ian had been with prior to being accepted into the RAF, still existed and it was these that supplied the desperately hoped for proof.

The joy I felt on receiving this news defies description; at last a huge weight seemed to have been lifted and I was filled with a sense of relief. My first reaction was to ring Mona in Australia but, this time, I remembered the time difference and managed to wait to pass on the news at a more appropriate hour. Now all that remained to do was to put matters in hand for the official funeral. So simple, I thought. Once again I was mistaken.

I spent some time talking to RAF Insworth to get information on the way forward; who needed to be contacted and who should be making which arrangements. There appeared to be an almost endless list of people who should be contacted, invited and generally informed.

I started with the relatives of the crew, then moved on to my friends, who had done so much, in Holland. The next contact was the military attaché in The Hague, Lt Col Le Hardy and his hard working secretary, Vicky Bant. I shall always be grateful to Vicky for her work and help prior to, during and immediately after the funeral. Now, having contacted all those who were to be at the heart of the ceremony, I began to look to those slightly farther afield. Ian's old squadron (101) needed to be contacted and also Sir Lewis Hodges, an ex commanding officer of 161 Squadron, plus many more; it seemed that the list was growing forever longer. It was when I called Sir Lewis to issue, at this stage, an unofficial invitation and to ask if he would take an active part in the service that another very strange coincidence occurred. During our conversation I mentioned my contact with Lt Col Le Hardy and Sir Lewis asked "Is that Christopher Le

TAKING THE WINGS OF THE MORNING

Hardy?" I confirmed that it was. Sir Lewis' reaction to this news was along the lines of "Good Heavens! He's my godson; I haven't seen him in years". How tangled this web of contacts was becoming.

Over the next few months, with many phone calls to Holland and Australia the ceremony began to take shape. I could never have imagined how much work and co-ordination went into organising a funeral with full military honours. Just a few of the organisations that needed to be contacted and kept informed were: RAF Insworth, The Commonwealth War Graves Commission, The British Embassy in the Hague and, of course, the many different Dutch authorities and services.

The structure of the service had to be considered and the wishes of Ian's sister, Mona, implemented and incorporated where possible. Ian's church had been Scottish Presbyterian and, therefore, we wanted a minister from that church to lead the service. This, of course, had to be approved by the minister and members of the church at Makkum where we wanted the ceremony to be held. We also thought it would be fitting to have a piper play at the service; one more task for the Colonel and Vicky to take on. Music, hymns and readings needed to be chosen and those whom we wished to deliver the readings asked if they would oblige. On top of all this the embassy had to arrange travel and accommodation for some of the guests and relatives; this too was not as straightforward as one might think. Mona was coming from Australia to stay with Helen and me for a few days prior to the funeral and, after this, flights had to be arranged for her and Helen to travel on to Holland. Once there transport needed to be organised to get them from Schiphol to the hotel, which was still to be booked; a hotel with enough rooms to accommodate all those who needed to stay plus extra rooms for those who only needed somewhere to change. On top of this it had to have enough room to hold the reception after the funeral.

Luckily, a local hotel, the Vigilante, in Makkum proved to be suitable. Arrangements made by the embassy were for the bearer party, supplied by RAF Laarbruch, to get to and from Makkum. Others that needed to be contacted and invited included local dignitaries and the relatives of the agents. Unfortunately, despite appeals in British newspapers, on radio and on local television I had been unable to trace a relative of one of the agents, Johannes Walter. A further duty for the embassy was to prepare and circulate the official press releases to the newspapers, radio and television. The amount of organisation, the attention to detail required and the sheer number of items that had to be considered was truly formidable. I just hoped that on the day everything would come together as neatly as it looked on paper. I need not have worried.

TAKING THE WINGS OF THE MORNING

My brother, Rick, and I travelled to Holland two days before the funeral as I was still in a state of some anxiety regarding the arrangements for the funeral and felt that I needed to be there to ensure that all was going smoothly.

On the evening of 20 October, Lt Col Le Hardy hosted a meal for a few of those who would be taking part in the following day's proceedings. There were, however, several interruptions during the meal as various people were called away to give interviews to the television reporters who had been allocated a room in the hotel for this purpose.

A few moments from the interviews stand out and are worth, I believe, a special mention. Of particular note is the one conducted, by a young reporter, with Mona. She was asked how she had heard about the finding of the wreck and the remains of her brother. Her reply was that I had rung her at 3 am (I had not considered the time difference). The reporter then pushed for what she obviously hoped would be an emotional reply, asking along the lines of "And what did you do when you heard the news?" Mona's reply must be a classical example of the unflappable British. She completely wrong footed the reporter when, in a very matter of fact tone, she said "I made a cup of tea and went back to bed".

TAKING THE WINGS OF THE MORNING

Sir Lewis Hodges gave an excellent description of what it had been like for the pilots and crews during those terrible years. Standing at the edge of the IJsselmeer with the waters lapping gently, the night dark and inhospitable, Sir Lewis paid tribute to the courage of these men, all risking their lives night after night to continue the fight in Europe.

My own interview has only embarrassing memories. One of the ladies present, at the request of the lighting manager, extracted a powder compact from her bag and proceeded to apply liberal amounts of powder to my glistening pate to stop the dazzle.

All in all it was a very pleasant evening but one could feel the underlying tension and apprehension of what the next day held in store for us all.

On the morning of the day of the funeral, 21 October, there was still an air of subdued expectancy and a certain amount of nervousness amongst those of us who had been staying in the hotel.

After breakfast Helen and I took both Mona and Sir Lewis Hodges to see the "Propeller Monument" at Exmorra. It was here that Sir Lewis confirmed that the aircraft had, indeed, been hit by cannon fire. When the hole in the propeller blade was pointed out to him, without any hesitation, he said that it had been caused by a 20 mm cannon shell. By this declaration he confirmed what I had believed, (although it went against the opinions of others); that the aircraft had not just flown into the Afsluitdijk, nor had it been brought down by "flak" but had been shot down by a night fighter (at this time the German air gunner had not been traced).

A short period was spent at the monument in quiet reflection, which must have been very emotional for Mona; not only being able to see and touch a part of her brother's aircraft but to realise the importance accorded to it by the people of Exmorra. From Exmorra it was just a short drive to the Kazematten museum where we were given a private viewing of an area of the museum that had been dedicated to those on board FK790.

Now it was back to the hotel Vigilante for lunch and more interviews before returning to the town for the funeral. We were completely in the hands of the British Embassy staff, the RAF and the people of Makkum; a very strange and somewhat disturbing feeling. For 13 years I had been leading the research into the loss of FK790 and now all control had been taken from me.

As Ian's immediate family Mona, Rick, Helen and I were taken to a small chapel where Ian's remains lay in a coffin, draped with the Union flag and surmounted by an RAF Officer's cap, for some moments of private thoughts and prayers. When we were ready, the RAF pall bearers and cap bearer were summoned and the procession from the chapel to the church began, led by a lone piper. Here I must pay tribute to those six pall bearers for the job they did. The wind was blowing in off the sea at almost gale force, (earlier it had brought down one of the four flagpoles), and they had a carry of some 400 metres at a slow march, with a heavy coffin, constantly buffeted by the wind, on their shoulders. They completed this march without faltering; thank you. Arriving at the church door I was surprised to a further two pipers playing, one on each side of the door.

Once inside the church the service began, conducted jointly by Drs. Ek and Rev. Gordon Craig. The opening remarks made by the Rev. Gordon Craig went a long way to ease the pain and some of the tension of the proceedings; I shall never forget them. He hinted that as a Scottish Presbyterian Ian should always have been in church on Sundays but was normally to be found on a golf course! "Well", he said *"finally* we have got you into church".

The rest of the service passed in a bit of a blur, the readings were delivered, prayers offered and hymns sung, along with some beautiful contributions from the local choir. For the pall bearers it was now back to work, no short carry from the church to graveside but a long, long slow march around the perimeter of the cemetery to the grave. Here with all due ceremony, standards from various organisations, including the Royal British Legion from Arnhem, wreath laying, the lone piper playing the chosen laments so beautifully and a bugler who played the "Last Post" Ian was finally, after 54 years, laid to rest alongside those of his crew. Late on parade, maybe, but together again.

Following the interment it was back to the hotel for the official reception. Here I met some of those from the Dutch authorities who had played such an important part in making the day possible, both by the work involved in the raising of the wreck and, most importantly, the successful identification of the remains.

During the course of the reception I discovered that the Dutch authorities had one or two surprises up their sleeves. First I was asked if a small silver penknife that had been found could have belonged to Ian. My reply was that if the blade was made of stainless steel it would, almost certainly, have been his; Ian's father had been a senior figure in one of the big steel works in Sheffield. Mona was called over and one of the Dutch officers presented her with the little penknife, which had been cleaned with such care as to look new, encased in its own presentation box.

Other parts of the aircraft were also handed to me to pass on to the relatives of the crew. Mrs. Pearson had already received the Morse key that her husband, Dennis, would have used. There was part of the navigator's lamp and other navigational items for the brothers of Kenneth Bunney, part of the gun turret for Derek Eliot, son of Eric Eliot the air gunner and various items from the cockpit for my brother and me. All these items had been cleaned, with great care, and mounted on wooden plinths, ready for display. The effort and thoughtfulness of the Dutch authorities went far beyond everyone's expectations; a very kind and sensitive gesture on their part which was greatly appreciated by all concerned.

The following morning I returned to the cemetery to get photographs of the many, many floral tributes that had been laid; not just by relatives and official organisations but also by private individuals who wished to show their respect. I was surprised and delighted to find that the headstone, organised by the Commonwealth War Graves Commission had, already, been set in place. The inscription, as requested by Mona, had been carved into the face of the stone and reads:

TAKING THE WINGS OF THE MORNING

HELD IN MEMORY DEAR
BELOVED BROTHER AND SON
PASSED INTO HIS PRESENCE
PEACE: HIS WORK WAS DONE.

So now the story was complete and the "Second ending" I referred to at the beginning had been achieved. However, I did not foresee that information would continue to come to light, certainly for the next three years, including a very major breakthrough.

WAS THAT

THE END?

TAKING THE WINGS OF THE MORNING

I said, at the beginning of this book, that the events, as they are written, are not necessarily in chronological order. Some of the information described in the preceding pages did not actually come to light until after the funeral. Also, as I said in the prologue, "How do you finish a story that, on one hand has ended and yet on the other hand has not"? Let me explain what I meant by this. In theory, with all the information that had come to light before October 1998, the burial of Ian's remains was the second ending, the first being the loss of the aircraft.

Some of the information that has come in since that date has answered many questions but, at the same time, begs answers for more.

In April 2001 I received word that the tail section of Ian's aircraft was to be "unveiled" as a monument to all those on board, at the Kazematten Museum, Kornwanderzand. In May of that year, Helen and I, along with all the other relations of the crew, were invited to attend. For some reason (I really do not know why) I decided to try, just once more, to find out what happened that night, 5/6 July 1944. I found a site on the Internet that appeared to deal with the type of enquiry I had in mind and so posted a message asking if anyone had any information at all regarding the events of that night.

TAKING THE WINGS OF THE MORNING

Within hours I had received four replies. Two said that they thought, as the aircraft had been flying so low, that it had hit the causeway (Afsluitdijk). These theories were refuted by Ron Morris, the other Hudson pilot from 161 Squadron who was also flying to Holland that night, when I spoke to him sometime later. Another said they thought the aircraft had been brought down by anti-aircraft fire; this is disproved by the horizontal hole made by a 20 mm cannon shell in the propeller blade. The fourth reply was from Huub van Sabben saying that he had taken a keen interest in this aircraft and the mystery surrounding it and he would help in any way he could. Having received this message I wasted no time in contacting Huub and, over the course of the next few days, exchanged much information with him. Huub said that he would take a fresh look at the records and within a day or two he came back saying that he had found an error in the records that had gone unnoticed for all those years.

There was a record of a night fighter action that night but the aircraft downed was not a Hudson and it had crashed near Rotterdam. This aircraft was thought to have been brought down by a Messerschmitt from Leeuwarden. Further checking proved this to be incorrect which now left a Messerschmitt in the right vicinity and at the right time with an acknowledged "kill". I do not know how he managed to do it but within ten days of my posting the original request for help Huub came up with the name and address of the one man from that Messerschmitt who survived the war. Huub immediately contacted me and asked if I wanted to contact the man. However, as I cannot speak German I asked Huub if he would make contact on my behalf, which he did. This is why I have been able to include the German side of the story regarding the downing of FK790.

I believe that the whole story of that tragic night will never be known, as so many questions still remain unanswered.

How did the Germans know the aircraft was coming?

Why, when Ron Morris says that they flew so low over the North Sea, was Ian's aircraft at a height where he could be attacked from *below?* Had something happened on board the aircraft that forced the pilot to gain height, thus showing up on the German Radar?

Many theories have been bandied about, even conspiracy theories, some of which have been quite plausible but are unproven. Perhaps one day some information will come to light and give the final ending to the story, until that day I leave you to draw your own conclusions as to what happened. The quest for information still continues.

GLOSSARY

BAT	Beam approach training
BBO	Bureau voor Bigzondere Opdrachten (Bureau of Special Operations)
CWGC	Commonwealth War Graves Commission
DFC	Distinguished Flying Cross
DSO	Distinguished Service Order
F/Lt	Flight Lieutenant
F/O	Flying Officer
F/Sgt	Flight Sergeant
FTS	Flying Training School
GEE	A radar navigation aid
HCU	Heavy Conversion Unit
Hfl	Dutch Guilders
ORB	Operational Record Book
OTU	Operational Training Unit
P/O	Pilot Officer
RVV	Raad van Verzet - Council of Resistance
Sgt	Sergeant

TAKING THE WINGS OF THE MORNING

Sqdn/Ldr	Squadron Leader
W/Cdr	Wing Commander
W/O	Warrant Officer
W/T	Wireless Telegraph